Tooshie

Defeating the Body Image Bandit

Cherrie Herrin-Michehl, MA, LMHC

Marietta,
you are
fearfully and
wonderfully made!
Psalms 139:14

Cherrie Herrin
Michehl

Table of Contents

Acknowledgements...7

Ch.1 You Know the Body Image Bandit Well 10

Ch.2 Body Image, Rejection, and Abandonment............15

Ch.3 Chasing "Skinny" 34

Ch.4 Faces and Masks...63

Ch.5 Birthdays. You Can't Live with 'Em, and You Can't Live Without 'Em –Or Can You? 80

Ch.6 Real Women Aren't Afraid to Wear Pink: Getting in Touch with Your Chickness 101

Ch.7 When Beauty Becomes a Beast............................113

Ch.8 Stalking the Fridge Substituting Food for Love.......128

Ch.9 Oh, to be a Kitty! 147

Ch.10 The Man on the Moon – No, I Mean the Chicken Diet 162

Ch.11 Mama Mia! How Mothers Influence Body Image.174

Ch.12 Entering the Abyss of Eatingdisorderville 191

Ch.13 Beware of Drunk Monkeys. Guarding Your Heart 199

Ch.14 Recognize, Reject, and Replace the Lies of the Body Image Bandit 212

Ch.15 Dance Your Life Song like a Diva.........................226

*To
George,
the lover of
my
soul.*

Man looks at outward appearance,
but God looks at the heart.

-1 Samuel 16:7

Acknowledgements

My husband, George, has been my greatest encourager. He waited patiently throughout this long journey as I fought two chronic illnesses while running a business, always supporting me and helping with household tasks. My parents also provided wonderful support and raised me to dream, to chase my goals and to pursue my passions. My sister, Kathy, helped support my writing journey by writing her own powerful story and encouraging me to cross the finish line.

A few years ago I learned about the importance of critique groups. My critique partners, Lydia E. Harris and Mindy Peltier, offered invaluable feedback. They helped me become not only a better writer, but have woven their own hearts into my soul. You are precious gifts from God.

Early in this writing process, I assembled a prayer team. I know prayer moves mountains. My heart is indebted to you prayer warriors: Sherry Bibb,

Karen Clem, Carol Corcoran, Sherri Davis, Amanda Jones, Joan Lockard, Kim Paul, Mindy Peltier, Kirsten Pyka, Sandy Saala (soon to be Amos), Jane Siegel, and Aunt Ellen Turner.

I would also like to thank my editor, Judy Bodmer, and Lynnette Bonner, my cover designer. Both played extremely important roles in bringing Tooshie to fruition.

Thank you also to all my friends who offered input on this book over the years. A special thank you to Hope T, Tanya H, Karen D, and Sherri D.

A special thanks to the school now called The Seattle School of Theology and Psychology. Your fingerprints deeply touch my essence and help me to see people through the powerful lens of story. I am forever grateful for your profound impact on my own life story.

Thank you to Gregory Jantz, Ph.D., for his encouragement and willingness to read the manuscript of an unknown writer, and for endorsing the book.

A special thank you also to Joyce Hart, Mick Silva, and Debbie Marrie. You all encouraged me to dance my life song like a diva.

I would never have accomplished this task

without the help from Jesus, my Lord and savior. I pray this book offers hope, and that it sets the captives free. To God be the glory. ~

Note: The people in this book are not real individuals. I have based the stories on a composite of hundreds of people I have met over the years.

Chapter 1

You Know the Body Image Bandit Well

What if you and your tooshie could finally make peace? You have dieted, exercised, and poured it into jeans three sizes too small. Maybe you, like me, bought a pair of yellow plastic bloomers designed to hook up to your vacuum cleaner and suck the fat off your hiney. Unfortunately, the Girl Scouts showed up during the procedure. Seeing you through the window, they were traumatized for life. You waddled to the door anyway and bought a year's supply of chocolate mint cookies.

Face it. Many of us spend enormous amounts of time dwelling on our derrieres. On some level, we believe the world actually cares about them, but in reality other people are too busy to ponder our plunder.

I imagine our love-hate relationship with food started in the Garden of Eden. Eve's hormones whacked out and she had a craving for chocolate that wouldn't quit, even though she had never tasted it. Bible scholars believe it wasn't a red delicious apple, but another type of fruit such as a persimmon. I think it may have been a large handful of chocolate beans, coffee beans, or hybrid chocolate-coffee beans that tasted like a mocha. Now that would certainly be tempting.

Can you picture Eve getting up on the wrong side of the hammock? Stepping out of the Tigris River after bathing, a bee buzzes by. She turns to swish it away with her long hair and sees for the first time one of the great wonders of the world: a woman's derriere in the reflection of the sunlit river. Realizing it belongs to her, she cries out, "Good gosh!" You've probably experienced similar thoughts in the mall while trying on jeans. *I had no idea my derriere was that expansive. I'd better do something about this thing before it gets totally out of control!*

The other possibility is that Eve argued with Adam the night before, and he lashed out with his tongue, saying, "Eve, you better do something about that derriere of yours or I'll ..." He never finished his sentence because he knew if he left Eve, the pickings

11

were slim, and he didn't know how he could work the garden without her to come home to at sundown. After all, television and remotes wouldn't be invented until much later.

Maybe part of Eve's desire to eat the fruit of the Tree of Knowledge of Good and Evil was the hope it would be the fad diet of her day. Somehow its fiber would operate like liposuction and she would have her dream body.

So began women's preoccupations with their bodies. Now don't pretend you don't know what I'm talking about because I know you do. You've exercised and dieted and some of you have binged, purged, and/or starved yourself in search of the perfect body, or a skinnier one or perhaps a less expansive model.

But if you actually succeeded in molding your dimensions into perfection, bizarre men started clinging to you like chocolate on chocolate-covered raisins. The fabulous derriere acted like a creep magnet, and wacky weirdoes came from everywhere to meet you because they loved your packaging. You resented this. This led you to drive through all the fast-food places in town and gorge yourself with sugary, fatty foods until you thought you would pop.

The bottom line is the more you obsessed about having the perfect packaging, the more you attracted guys who wanted you for your looks and not your heart.

Perhaps you've worried about how your body measures up to airbrushed standards of models and movie stars who are eaten from within by the beasts of bulimia and anorexia. Eating disorders form an imploding black hole that—without proper treatment— always end in darkness and have swallowed up many lives due to heart failure and other health complications.

This book is for anyone who has been weighed down with feelings about body image. You will experience more joy when you realize God is much more concerned about your heart than your derriere. Of course you already know this in your head; but when you truly believe it in every cell of your body, you will win more battles in the war against the Body Image Bandit. Finally, you will learn some tactics to protect yourself from the Bandit – the Enemy, the Accuser, and the Father of Lies, who continually works to convince you that your value comes from outer beauty as opposed to inner beauty. We are drowning in a tsunami of cultural messages that say,

"To be thin is to be beautiful, and beauty is everything." The truth is, "Man looks at outward appearance, but God looks at the heart" (1 Samuel 16:7).

The intent of this book is not to resolve eating disorders, but to help people begin to love the bodies God gave them. Beyond that my hope is we learn to focus more important questions than "Do these jeans make my rearie look big?"

The people in this book are not real individuals. They represent a composite of individuals I have worked with and known over the years.

Although I am a licensed mental health counselor, I do not specialize in eating disorders. If you have an eating disorder, I highly recommend you seek professional help from a counselor with significant experience and training in eating disorders. Some excellent resources are:

www.nationaleatingdisorders.org

www.aplaceofhope.com

Chapter 2

Body Image, Rejection,

and Abandonment

Age is starting to catch up with me. My skin is turning saggy and baggy, and my hair is growing the color of steel. Doesn't it know the DVD was called, "Buns of Steel," not "Hair of Steel"? Sometimes my hairdresser secretly snips each strand out while engaging me in conversation, so I resemble a patchwork porcupine. Finally she gave up, and a whole village of granite hair stares back at me in the mirror.

These innocent-looking gray hairs are actually rebellious adolescents in disguise. Besides turning smoky they double in thickness and develop attitudes. The little dudes grew wiry and do whatever they feel like. So even if you have a cute style, your head is covered with a splattering of gray hairs all doing their own things, boinging up toward the sky with twisted necks. What looks like a mop turning gray in reality is rebellion confined to your scalp.

Rebellion confined to the scalp is not nearly as serious as the more critical issue, which is rebellion of the heart. All of us—if we have the courage to be completely honest—are committed to protecting ourselves from harm in our relationships. We have been deeply wounded by other people and have vowed in our hearts to do whatever it takes to avoid being hurt again. On some level, we have decided to protect ourselves from relational pain regardless of the costs. This promise to guard ourselves from vulnerability is rebellion of the heart. We protect ourselves to the point that we are insulated not only from the pain of relationships but from the beauty of relationships as well. This creates a deep well of loneliness that is hard to escape.

Since we were created for relationship – with God and with other people – we derail when we put other activities ahead of relationships. We may pretend God designed us for other purposes, such as workaholism, stacking up wealth, having fun, or checking things off to-do lists. The truth that we were created for relationships slides down to the bottom of our priorities, which topples our balance on the teeter-totter of life.

We have expended great amounts of energy to avoid the enemy Abandonment and her close cousin, Rejection. The commitment to avoid being abandoned plus the obsession about thinness and beauty in our culture create a fertile soil for eating disorders. Virtually every American woman, even if she doesn't struggle with an eating disorder, has disliked her body at one time or another. Self-contempt and specks of hatred for one's body are as common as chocolate chips in chocolate chip cookie dough.

Women have been duped into believing if they have perfect bodies, they will have great friends, wonderful mates, fabulous careers, and happy lives. The media pitches the message that beauty is the major answer to life's problems for women. This plants seeds of deep insecurity as advertisements brainwash us into thinking good looks will lock out Abandonment and Rejection forever.

Some bulimics start purging and/or exercising obsessively after feeling rejected. Rejection and Abandonment play starring roles, springing people into the arms of the Body Image Bandit. The Bandit eats away at their body images like a bus load of women eating their way through Baskin Robbins after going off their diets.

We live in a culture in which size 12 and 14 models are called, "Plus size." Is it any wonder that girls feel the pressure to be thin when they are young? "I'm too fat," "I'm too short," or "My body isn't curvy enough," are typical self-talk phrases that live in women's heads. Another layer of lies includes expectations about facial beauty. The messages we are supposed to have no flaws in our hair, skin, eyes, and lips are juxtaposed upon an already poisoned body image. Included in this satchel of lies are issues about our faces not matching up to the media standards, such as, "My lips are too thin."

These poisonous media messages sink into our skin, through our pores, and into our hearts until we feel we are not good enough. This reaches into the deepest crevasses of our souls, making us feel unlovable and insignificant. The darkest shadow inside this dreadful cloud of despair is the fear we are unlovable.

My own abandonment and rejection issues became gouged into my soul at the unripe age of eleven when my family moved from a rainy, sleepy town in Washington State to the beach town of Kihei, Maui, Hawaii.

Dad plopped a 16-ounce plastic Tupperware cup onto the carpet of the long, skinny hall of the trailer we lived in while building our own house as a family. He practiced sinking golf balls into the bottom of the cup until it became as concave as a contact lens. He said he needed to develop his skills to play on Maui. As an estimator and superintendent of a construction company outside of Seattle, he bid on a job to repair the sewer system in Kihei. We couldn't wait to hear if the company won the job. The days dragged on as slowly as a Northwest slug for several weeks until dad received a call that the company won the bid.

I grabbed a bath towel, tied it around my T-shirt and jeans into a makeshift hula skirt, and pretended to hula dance as I hummed what sounded to me like a Hawaiian song. Gusts of wind howled through the rain-drenched window and tried to dampen our party, but we didn't care. We were about to move to Paradise, where the sun would always shine on our backs, the warm blue water would welcome us, and bad things never happened. Or so we thought.

I doodled palm trees, sunny skies, and surfers

while watching pregnant raindrops slide down my bedroom window in Fall City, Washington. Years before Microsoft set up shop a handful of miles away, the little town was a small logging community. Nowadays it drips with money, but back then humble loggers' homes stood where estates now house Microsoft employees. One of the richest men in the world lives a half hour away. In 1974 I was sick of sloshing through the mud and rain, stepping carefully so as not to squish slug guts underfoot as I walked a half mile to school.

My sixth-grade class threw a surprise going away party for me, complete with a piñata, dancing, and oodles of Christmas cookies since it was mid-December. They presented me with a refrigerator-sized box wrapped in lemon yellow paper. Inside nested a series of boxes descending in size, also wrapped in sunny yellow paper. The smallest box was a necklace box containing $21.55, which was a lot of money for loggers' children to collect back then. Mr. Wright, my teacher, told me the money was to buy a surfboard when I arrived in Paradise. About a week after I got to Maui, I wrote them a thank-you note directly on a coconut with a black felt marker and mailed it to them without a box.

Whales spouted and pounded their enormous powerful tails against the brilliant azure water as I approached my new school across the street from the beach. I scanned the horizon for shark fins. I didn't realize I was about to enter into shark-infested waters, but they would be inside the school.

When I opened the door of my homeroom class, a sea of eyes glared at me with contempt. A few students snickered, whispered, and pointed at me. A gust of silence fell upon the classroom, and I didn't realize I had just entered into a culture clash of the Pacific Northwest and Maui. Thankfully, soon after I arrived, the recess bell rang. Raindrops beat down on the rich red playground soil. (I wouldn't understand until later most kids skipped school when rain fell from the normally blue sky.)

A group of eight or nine native girls approached me as I walked onto the field. Their leader stopped about six inches away from me and glared into my face. I had been so excited to interact with people of other cultures, as Fall City was mostly a Caucasian community, and I wanted friends of all races. I was not ready for my first encounter with prejudice.

"*Eye haole* (white person)," the leader spoke, with hatred spilling out of each word. "Get da hell offa dis island, white girl. You no belong hea. Go back to da mainland whea you belong."

Her Pidgin English warned me to go back to the Mainland. The rest of the pack behind her glared, as if they could bore a hole through my bleeding heart.

I don't remember how I responded, but only how that first day started a landslide of hatred directed toward me because of my blonde hair, pale skin, and blue eyes. For about a year and a half, I attended a school in which I was despised for my white skin. There were only a handful of other Caucasian kids at the school, and I blended in like a Washington red delicious apple in a pile of papayas.

One day when I arrived at school, I noticed the native kids wearing white bands around their arms. Soon I learned the bands signified Kill Haole Day, in which one white person was chosen to be beaten until he or she was just this side of consciousness. I wasn't "chosen," but a friend of mine in the local high school was. The students prepared to crush his skull with a cement block when the principal walked around the corner just in time to save his life.

I ached to be accepted for who I was. But as the Hawaiian sun kissed my golden hair, it grew lighter and lighter. My heart grew as dark and cold as the ancient lava rock that had hardened to form the island of Maui.

Abandonment, fear, and rejection ravaged through me like a delicate jellyfish blown into oblivion by a tidal wave. Eventually my parents gave in and sent me to a private school, although the expense burdened them. But the vivacious, bubbly girl that boarded the flight from Seattle to Hawaii crawled into a cave and became consumed with fear.

Two years later, we moved back to Fall City. But I was no longer cheerful. Enduring almost two years of abuse due to my light coloring turned me into a quiet, withdrawn, and depressed teenager. My sun-drenched platinum blonde hair, deep golden tan, and filled-out figure made me stand out.

My commitment to self-protection from the pain of relationships started with a desire to fade into the background. I spoke little and tried to be invisible. Due to my curvy figure, sun blazed blonde hair, and rich golden tan, this wasn't easy. Almost everyone else had pale winter skin.

After a while I got tired of being invisible and decided to be funny at times. The problem with being funny was that people didn't take me seriously when I did have something to say, even if it was small talk about something like hair.

My hair has been many different colors including chestnut, auburn, and all shades of blonde. One day a friend asked me what my natural hair color is. I couldn't remember. The general shade used to be called dishwater blonde, which is certainly not a flattering phrase. I picture dirty sink water at the end of Thanksgiving dinner where food particles dance and water ski on top of the greasy grimy surface.

I usually keep my hair fairly short, as in shoulder length or shorter, but decided to grow it long about eight years ago. My hair is thick, but each strand is skinny, just like my earlobes and fingernails. (Those are the only skinny body parts I have, and I inherited them from my mother.) I grew my hair until it was almost to my elbows, which I enjoyed because I could change styles often.

Growing my hair long took every ounce of patience I could muster, and then some. Many times during the grueling process, I almost whacked it off because I got tired of the painful act of growing it out. I really wish there was a hair hotline for people to call when they are about ready to get out the weed whacker or dog clipper and whack it all off.

"Hair Hotline. Is this a hair emergency?"

"Yes, it is," I assure Ms. Hair. "I've been growing my hair out for months, and I'm about ready to take a weed eater to it. My bangs hang halfway down my eyes and poke me like little kids tickling their younger brother. It's really annoying. I've tried gel, mousse, and every type of hairspray on the planet, including pizza-flavored. But that only resulted in a crowd of teenage boys hanging around my house."

"Oh, ma'am, that sounds pretty heavy."

"That's not the worst part," I say. "Last week I gave it all up and globbed a chunk of Crisco on my hair to try to get it under control, and now I look ridiculous. I can't get it out of my hair. I've tried everything I can think of."

Ms. Hair snickers. Just what I need – an unfriendly hair hotline helper to shame me.

"I'm sorry," she says. "I was reading the funniest email someone sent me."

"It looks pretty bad, and people have been calling me Crisco Head and telling me I should get into the oil export business. They are right; I look like I could resolve the entire world oil crisis. I really need help."

"Sounds serious. Maybe you could do the export thing, or get a wig."

I can't believe her suggestions. "Don't you have any other ideas?" I ask with a sigh.

"There is one other thing. Buy a box of cornmeal and empty the entire contents on your head. Rub it into your roots, making sure it covers every strand. Then brush it out. Your hair will look sleek and gorgeous."

"Sounds good. I'm gonna go buy some cornmeal right now."

I zip to the store in my older convertible, hoping the wind will whip through my bird's nest-like hair. But of course that's impossible. At the stoplight, I reach into my bag and get out my lipstick to do a quick touch-up.

Climbing out of the car, I notice a giant grease stain on the headrest. I whip out my compact mirror and realize I have applied a thick layer of flesh-colored cover up instead of my favorite lipstick. My lips are heavily covered with the cover-up because I decided to apply the lipstick extra thick to detract from my greasy hair.

I pull out a Kleenex and wipe off the cover-up, then strut into the baking section of the grocery store to grab some cornmeal. I pay for it, drive home, race into the kitchen, and pour the entire box on my head. That's when the phone rings.

My husband calls to let me know we will be having guests over for dinner. He says his boss had to fly to Australia unexpectedly to take care of some business, so the dinner party scheduled for next week has to take place that night–at our house.

"That's gonna be a little tough," I respond. Later we will definitely have a long chat about this.

"Oh, don't let it stress you out, honey. You know Bob is from Oklahoma and loves a good Southern meal with lots of grease and cornmeal – something like beans and cornbread, with lots of bacon grease in the beans." Ugh.

"Well, okay, I guess I'll head to the store and grab some beans and cornmeal." Or maybe I could just extract it from my head, I think.

"It's been such a lovely evening," Cindy, Bob's wife, comments. "A delicious meal, great company, and I didn't even have to cook." She winks at me, then starts to closely examine my hair as we walk to the front door to see them off. "You know, Cherrie, I have to say your hair looks stunningly beautiful. You treated yourself to that new spa they advertised on TV, didn't you?"

"Oh, no, I didn't," I insist.

"Whatever you put on your hair –I want to get some for myself. Share your little secret with me."

"Really I can't. I mean it's just regular stuff I found around the house, nothing special or expensive."

They finally leave, and I race down the hall to look in the mirror. Cindy is right. My hair looks better than ever.

People think short hair is easy to style, but actually long hair takes much less time. When I wear short hair, every morning I looked like a rabid rooster when I crawled out of bed. My hair smashed and looked like I super glued it to the side of my head. People called me Rooster Head on camping trips because I didn't have time to fluff it out before breakfast.

After about four years of wearing my hair long, I got tired of it. So I had it cut about six inches shorter. I thought it looked spunky and trendy, but nobody commented. We all know what that means, don't we? It looks like the contents of the old Tupperware container you found in the fridge the last time you cleaned it out.

When women pass forty, some of them try to

pull their long hair back into ponytails very tightly in order to smooth out the wrinkles on their faces. I can tell you from experience it doesn't work, and you will only give yourself a headache. Maybe people are more committed to keeping their long hair now because forty is the new thirty, seventy is the new sixty, and ninety is the new eighty. I guess that is how they figure. Somehow it doesn't all add up. But what do I know?

Years ago, I was young and unaware of the truth that God cares more about how well we love others than how well we look. I obsessed about my appearance and dedicated myself to improving it whenever I caught myself in a reflection, whether it was a toaster or a mirror. If I would have been able to understand where my true value comes from, life would have been less stressful. Life would have been much less about my hair, skin color, and other physical characteristics. Decades passed before I realized my real value comes from my heart. I was buying into the cultural messages thrown at me by the world. These messages are the deceptions of the Enemy, the Father of Lies, whom I call the Body Image Bandit.

The Lies of the Body Image Bandit:

1.   Appearance is almost everything. God values our hearts more than the size of our hips. The Bible emphasizes the heart above all else and encourages us to develop the qualities of Christ: Galatians 5:22 says, "But the fruit of the spirit is love, joy, peace, patience, kindness, goodness, faithfulness, and self-control (NIV).

2.   Thinness and height are two major criteria of beauty. God's Word, however, emphasizes caring for the bodies we were born with. Obviously God likes variety, as he created different body types, ethnicities, and heights. Romans 12:1b tells us, "Offer your bodies as living sacrifices, holy and pleasing to God – this is your spiritual act of worship."

3.   Fat is bad. Our society frowns upon fat to the point of encouraging women to become ultra-thin. However, a certain amount of fat allows women to bear and nurse children. When women become ultra-thin, they stop menstruating and are unable to become pregnant. Proverbs 31, which is a classic passage of womanhood, clearly states,

"Her arms are strong for her tasks." This implies that she isn't stick thin.

4. Food is the enemy; it creates fat. God created a variety of foods to be enjoyed in moderation to nourish our bodies. 1 Timothy 4:4 explains, "For everything God created is good, and nothing is to be rejected if it is received with thanksgiving."

5. Beauty is completely external. Scripture emphasizes internal beauty as opposed to the external beauty our culture worships. The New Testament, in particular, rates internal beauty much higher than external beauty. 1 Peter 3:3 states, "What matters most is not your outer appearance – the styling of your hair, the jewelry you wear, the cut of your clothes – but your inner disposition" (The Message).

6. Youth is beautiful and old age is ugly. The interesting fact is the Bible says we should greatly value the elderly. Proverbs 16:31 tells us, "Gray hair is a crown of splendor, it is attained by a righteous life" (NIV). Another powerful verse is Job 12:12,

which says, "Is not wisdom found among the aged? Does not long life bring understanding?"

Looking back, I wish I would have known there are different standards of beauty throughout the world. These also change throughout history. For example, you may have thought that the 1980s were the big hair days, or that Texas used to be the Big Hair State. (Can't you just picture the phrase on their license plates?)

In pre-revolutionary France, for example, the trendy look was hair that reached six feet high and contained bird's nests, fruit, and flowers. Imagine strolling along the beach, seagulls fighting over the cranberries in your hair. Then you notice a supremely rotten smell, and realize it's coming from the mid-section of your hair. You forgot to take out the kiwi fruit and pineapple from two weeks ago. And you thought the eighties big hair drove you batty.

Actually, the seventies and eighties were my decades because I could go from 5'3" (almost) to 5'10" from my big hair and platform shoes. Ah ... those were the days!

What would happen if we could completely grasp that God cares much more about our hearts than our hair? On the surface we probably understand, but most of us could do better at understanding the scripture, "Man looks at outward appearance, but God looks at the heart." I hope and pray that those words become branded onto our hearts, and that we can reclaim the plunder of the Body Image Bandit.

Chapter 3

Chasing "Skinny"

I hadn't seen my friend Rebecca in over a year, and as we sat sipping coffee, I prayed I wouldn't stare at her lips, which had quadrupled in size since the last time I saw her. I could feel my gaze slipping from her eyes onto the pair of pink slugs resting just above her chin.

Some people are born with full, beautiful lips. Not Rebecca. She always had thin little lipettes, until today. They used to barely appear on her face, but now they had their own reality show.

Cotton candy colored sparkly lip gloss gave The Lips a larger-than-life look. I noticed people shielding their eyes from the glare. Bubble-gum pink lip liner gave The Lips a multi-dimensional reality. Apparently she had slapped on a jar of Vaseline to finish off the look. I couldn't believe she could talk with all the gunk on her lips. It was a miracle. I half expected The Lips to get stuck together, and then I would have to call 911. I slipped into a daydream...

"Emergency Services. How can I help you?"

Breathing heavily, I gasp for air. "It's my friend Rebecca," I sputter.

"What's the problem, ma'am?"

"It's her lips." There. I manage to get it out.

"Her *lips?*"

"Yes, that's right. Her lips are stuck together, and—"

"Did she accidentally swallow Elmer's glue? That happens to a lot of first graders."

"No, I think she wanted to have voluminous, movie-star lips and had a lip job, then piled on truckloads of lip gloss, lip liner, and Vaseline to get the fullest look possible. Now she can't pry them apart."

"Okay, this is obviously a prank call, and I'm gonna have to report you." Click.

"Cherrie, hello, are you listening?" Rebecca woke me from my dream. "For a minute it looked like you were off in your own little world."

Oops. I guess she could talk after all.

As we continued our visit, I realized I wasn't present with Rebecca, something I struggled with before I attended graduate school. I used to be off in my own head during conversations, thinking about what to make for dinner, where to go kayaking, or what color to paint my bathroom. All the while people thought I was really tracking with them. Then I learned the importance of being present with all people as much as possible.

Much as I tried, The Lips distracted me. I wanted to ask her what she'd done to them, but didn't want to embarrass her.

I tried to get fuller lips on several occasions using various over-the-counter products. They worked well and made my lips dazzle. The problem was when I tried to talk, eat, or drink the goop that fattened my lips slid out of the corners of my mouth. I could wear the lip enhancer as long as I didn't open my mouth. My lips looked movie starrish, but I had to be completely silent. That kind of took the fun out of it.

Driving home from the coffee shop, I thought about the hundreds of conversations about body image that come up when I counsel women. No matter why they initially make their appointment, most women eventually express dissatisfaction with their bodies. A few name displeasure with their lips. But many believe if they attain a certain size or weight, they will achieve happiness and their problems will dissolve. Some exercise until their joints hurt every waking moment as well as when they're asleep. They fit society's standard of beauty, but they ache like a hundred-year-old woman from working out hour upon hour for years on end.

Often clients start counseling because of current relationship struggles. Unbeknownst to them, they are repeating a similar plot they lived as children. For example, a person who grew up in a wealthy home with loving parents but a mother who worked seventy hours per week married a man who seemed like a solid person. However, years after walking down the aisle, she realizes her husband is like her mother. Not in personality, but in the way the husband is unavailable because his priorities are workaholism or his inability to be faithful. One way people deal with stress is to self-medicate with food. That's why "When did you start to gain weight" is a pivotal question. Often it's after sexual abuse, or during a stormy relationship or other traumatic experience.

I ran into a former client a few years ago at a grocery store, and noticed she had lost a significant amount of weight. Nobody was nearby, so we started talking about it, and she said she had dropped about eighty pounds. I asked how she did it, and she explained most of her weight loss came from working on her internal struggles in our counseling sessions. This happened even though we had rarely devoted counseling time to food or weight issues. The weight gradually came off as she processed the difficult parts of her life story. She gradually lost her desire to self-medicate with food. For her, the pain from childhood was her parents' divorce.

If you would have asked her before entering counseling, she would have said her parents' divorce happened so many years ago, it didn't affect her anymore. She didn't realize she'd developed a relational style which she pulled into her own marriage as well as other relationships. Many people like her play what I call Diet-Binge Ping-Pong. They diet for a period of time, then develop intense cravings, and then binge because they feel deprived. This leads, once again, to shame. So they start another diet and do the same back and forth game repeatedly.

Women in developed nations tend to judge their bodies brutally. They battle a gnawing desire to be thin. If you notice how often you hear women talking about food, fat, working out, sizes, diets, calories, and their bodies, you'll understand how deeply the desire to be thin is entrenched into our culture. Make a note of each time you hear a woman talk about wanting to lose weight, size, or dissatisfaction with her body. You may not be able to get through a week – let alone a day or two – without hearing one talk of such topics. This language is called, "fat talk."

This hyper-focus on thinness causes women to develop monumental amounts of shame and self-contempt for their bodies. Usually this starts when they experience some type of traumatic experience, such as the divorce of their parents, a breakup with a boyfriend, or moving. I'm not saying these events cause body image issues, but bumps along life's road can lead people to self-medicate. This can cause them to leap into the arms of their drug of choice for comfort. Often, this is food. This overeating results in weight gain, which leads them to dislike their bodies at a deeper level since thin bodies are idolized. The media provides a powerful soil for this self-contempt. And sometimes parents, teachers, and coaches spread fertilizer on this weed garden. Since our culture worships thinness, this scene is commonplace.

Some women (and men) are addicted to beating themselves up with the message they don't measure up. They hear this message as children, whether it's about school work, lack of athletic ability,

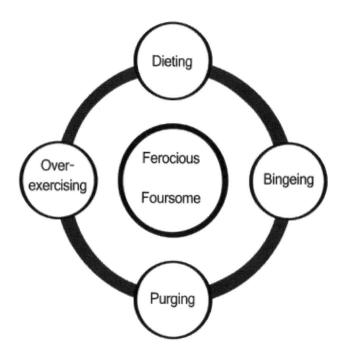

appearance, or other aspects of their lives. This spills over to the point that if nobody expresses disdain, the thoughts and comments continue in their heads. They become so comfortable with the shame, they feel naked without it.

This shame and self-contempt leads girls and

women into the contemptuous cycle I call the Ferocious Foursome. The Ferocious Foursome may include dieting, bingeing, purging (for some), and/or excessive exercising (for some).

Some women play diet-binge ping pong. By this, I mean they go back and forth from dieting to bingeing.

Typically, the girl feels fat, even though she may be within the normal weight or body composition limits. This is important because many of the girls in this phase don't qualify as overweight to begin with. They have been brainwashed by our society into thinking thin is their ticket to a perfect life. So they scrutinize their bodies and find excess fat, or what they believe is excess fat.

By age four or five, most girls already feel that any plumpness is bad. Sadly, the media fails to mention that some fat is normal and will enable them to have babies much later, as well as nurse their children and carry them on their hips. Another fact the media fails to mention is that breast tissue naturally contains a large percentage of fat. Sometimes women express a desire to wear a tiny size of clothes and have relatively large breasts at the same time. I explain to them that doesn't usually happen naturally because breast tissue contains a great deal of fat.

The end result of the brainwashing – as well as photo shopping – of the media is that little girls end up feeling that all fat is bad, whether it is on their bodies or in food. So of course they naturally fall prey to the first phase of the Ferocious Foursome, which is dieting.

When did you first begin to diet? Dieting has become a rite of passage for teen girls. Whether the first attempt ends in success or failure, it likely gives them a taste where they long for more. If they lose weight, they become believers, and if not, they profess to try again and again until they get it "right".

Just when they begin to feel sure-footed from the triumph of dieting, the ground shifts beneath them, bumping them onto the merry-go-round of self-contempt. They feel completely deprived, and begin to crave what they have started to call *bad* foods. This turns them into eating machines. The hunger wells up within them like a hurricane ready to ravage everything in its path. Suddenly they crave fatty, sweet, and salty foods like never before. They can't get enough and feel as though they must eat everything because hunger consumes them. Food, food, food, is on their minds a great majority of their waking hours and sometimes in their dreams as well. They have opened the floodgates of eternal hunger. They crave foods that they love, as well as foods that they did not used to like before they felt deprived from dieting.

They now feel insatiably starved, which leads to the first all-out binge. The binge fools their hearts into happiness, but only briefly. Finally, their hearts free-fall into the shaft of despair and depression, with waves of guilt and shame knocking them into the heart of hopelessness. They spin on the merry-go-round of self-loathing, dizzy and depressed from a level of hopelessness they never knew possible.

During my sophomore year in high school, I wanted to lose five to ten pounds. I felt the only way to do it was to go on a diet. I was an athlete and loved to exercise, so I felt the only other thing I needed to do was go on a diet. Now that is an interesting phrase, because if you go *on a diet,* you imply that you will eventually go off.

I mentioned to my dad I was starting a diet, and he said it was a bad idea. First, he didn't think I was fat. Secondly, he thought if I wanted to lose a few pounds I should just "cut back a little." I looked at him as if he had three heads. "Dad, are you *serious?*" I asked. I continued to educate him. "Everyone knows that doesn't work." I shook my head in disbelief, wondering how he could be so naive on such an important subject. Dad obviously hadn't spent enough time reading beauty and fashion magazines, and his lack of knowledge showed.

I realized years later that my first diet had launched me onto the escalator of the Ferocious Foursome. I don't remember what kind of a diet I went on, but I do remember the intense cravings. So I went from the first phase of the Ferocious Foursome, dieting, to the second phase of the Ferocious Foursome, which is bingeing.

The cravings started a millisecond after I decided to start my diet. I hadn't even begun the official "diet" when the mammoth cravings began. I decided mid-week I would go on a diet, but of course planned to start the following Monday. You know exactly what I'm talking about, don't you? Apparently there is an unofficial commandment, "Thou shalt start dieting on Monday." Simply telling myself I was going to *begin* dieting started the craving monster within to grow. Thinking I would never eat yummy foods again led to an all-out binge, which I had rarely experienced before I decided to go "on" my first diet.

Even while not bingeing, I began eating more than my normal quantities of food. First of all, I had no rules about eating before my diet started. I ate what I wanted when I wanted, and since I loved exercising I'd never been overweight more than a few pounds. But once I drowned myself in teen beauty and fashion magazines, I began to think of myself as flawed because I was born with a muscular body type and loved sports. God had created my body athletic and curvy.

I stuffed my mind with magazine articles about what to eat and not eat. I learned about evil foods the diet experts said to avoid entirely. These included sweets, bread, and potatoes. I had a sweet tooth the size of a semi-truck, but didn't care much about bread, and enjoyed potatoes in moderation.

The magazines blasted me repeatedly with messages that my body was unacceptable. My petite, athletic body was not the type that adorned beauty and fashion magazines. Often when girls and women look at fashion magazines, they feel discouraged. I was no different, although I wouldn't have been able to see the connection.

Once I learned about so-called "bad" foods, I craved them. I even started to want foods I never liked much before. As a little girl I wasn't too fond of peanut butter, white cake, or doughnuts. But once I learned about the official list of bad foods, I started to crave these foods. Sometimes I wonder if I would have craved Brussels sprouts if they had been on the list of forbidden foods. It's hard to imagine since I would rather get hung by my toenails than eat that particular vegetable, but still I wonder. For example, I've always loved chocolate, but can't remember craving chocolate until I started dieting.

The cravings became fueled by my all-or-nothing (also called black and white) thinking. Either I was "on" a diet, or "off" a diet. I propelled into a cycle which created its own momentum, almost as if I was spinning around on a merry-go-round at a high velocity, and wanted to jump off but couldn't.

The diet worked for a while, but the truth is diets aren't long-term solutions. People who lose weight more often than not gain it all back, plus more, over time. I know of only two people who have lost a significant amount of weight and kept it off for two decades or more. Yes, some people do it, but they are as rare as chocolate-covered pickles.

You are probably more likely to be run over by a Hershey's chocolate truck than you will go on a diet and keep the weight off for the rest of your life, let alone a decade.

Dieting can easily develop into an addiction. Friends and relatives praise women when they lose weight, much more than most other achievements. But the problem is the more you diet, the more you crave foods you normally would have eaten in small amounts. Mark Twain expressed the same concept about his problem with smoking. "Giving up smoking is the easiest thing in the world. I know because I've done it thousands of times," he said.

I finally began to understand dieting becomes an undertow like the momentum of the ocean when it decides to roll out another glorious wave. First it gets psyched up by gathering thousands of gallons of water. Once it collects the bountiful row of water, the wave curls upon itself and throws the water back to shore with magnificent power.

The same holds true with dieting. You invest loads of time and energy into counting calories, fat grams, and/or carbohydrates. On a Monday you start the diet that is going to make you skinny and give you the perfect life. So you pork out until you've almost outgrown all of your jeans because you're a free woman or man until Monday. Then on Monday your all-or-nothing thinking kicks into turbo mode and you have a good (perfect or close to perfect) dieting day. You think you're on your way to skinnihood, and you will have an amazing life because of your new skinny body.

But by Thursday or Friday, the cravings build up until you can't stand it another minute and eat everything not nailed down. You pack your gut with all the foods you hungered after. The binge is a violent experience in which you shove the food in like an abandoned dog that hasn't eaten in a week. You do this either alone or with one or more of your dieting buddies who have also bought into the cultural lie: "If I am skinny, I will have the perfect life." Once again, you are scared that if you don't stop this pattern, your weight will double and you will grow sad and lonely. So you hop back on the diet train, but all you can think about is food and the tiny jeans you will buy. Once again, your brain saturates with thoughts about food, fat, and your new, skinny life. You go to stores, restaurants, your cupboards, and graze your way through Costco again and again until they figure out you've devoured all the samples and kick your rear end out.

Overeaters Anonymous works on our life stories, which is why many who work their 12-step program keep the weight off. Once again, this illustrates how weight problems are more often than not about pain in our lives.

"These are *samples*," said the Costco sample lady, "not your entire *dinner*. If you want *dinner*, go to the food court and buy a whole cooked pizza." She gave me the evil eye, and I stopped myself from stealing her last three sample meatballs (the best in the entire country, I might add).

"A great idea," I said, just to get back at her. I wanted to stick my tongue out at her, but remembered I am a Christian and am supposed to be nice. Walking away, I considered buying a gigantic pizza and stuffing it in my mouth. At that moment, I craved everything. Except, of course, Brussels sprouts.

Too embarrassed to buy a pizza by this time, I hopped in my car, drove to the closest fast food restaurant, and ordered a number one. I gobbled it down while driving until my shirt had mayonnaise and grease spots all over it. Then I remembered the best ice cream shop in town around the corner and ordered a super scooper sundae through the drive-through.

I bet you've had a similar experience. Once you wolfed down the greasy number one and the super scooper sundae faster than you can say "monster cookie," you decide it doesn't matter anymore. You are an all-or-nothing thinker, which you learned when you grew up. You might as well eat everything. Once again, the all-or-nothing thinking kicks into high gear, causing you to eat absolutely everything you ever wanted. You have entered into the realm of the All-Out Binge. (Sadly enough, the latest research shows this phase includes excessive drinking. Many young women, in their dieting flings, are so concerned about calories they avoid food altogether and substitute alcohol.)

Then shame consumes your soul and you fall backwards, once again into the arms of self-contempt and the Body Image Bandit. Now you feel some hatred toward yourself for gorging down more food than a whole barnyard of pregnant cows could eat in a week. Which reminds you, you certainly feel like a cow. Ugh.

One of my journeys through the jungle of weight loss led me to a weight-loss clinic. Out of desperation, I joined this outfit one summer. I did pretty well and lost about twelve pounds, which is a lot for me because of my height. I only had about three pounds to go until I reached my goal. I felt discouraged because I plateaued and no more weight was coming off. During the end, each time I got weighed by the Diet Police Force lady, she glared at me. "Hmmm...you haven't lost anything in a few weeks. In fact you've been going up and down," she said with a scowl. I happened to notice she looked larger than me, although we were about the same height. She glared at me.

"Yeah, it's a lot harder at the end," I said.

"What's taking you so long? You only need to lose three more pounds. I could do that in a weekend." She wagged her finger in my face, and the fatty deposits under her arm jiggled in agreement.

"Hey, I'm doing the best I can," I said.

"Apparently that's not good enough, is it?" Shame was her drug of choice, and she felt powerful in her position.

I walked away and sat down to listen to another

member of the Diet Police Force instruct us to eat more fresh vegetables and less brownies. *Duh.* Once again, I realized these matters are about the heart. I longed for a program that would address the issues of my heart, because I realized I was dealing with a mild food addiction.

The center of addiction is trauma as well as genetics. When the trauma is not dealt with, people continue to fill the heart pain with pizza, chips, and cookie dough. Since that time I have been actively in a twelve step program, which is a beautiful way of life, and also helps me with the matters of the heart.

After the discussion on what to eat and what not to eat, I left the building knowing I would never see the Diet Police Force again. On the way home, I stopped at the closest fast food restaurant and ordered a number one. I knew it contained so much fat that my arteries would get clogged up just looking at it. But oh, did it fill me up, but a second later I felt myself fall back down the elevator shaft into the bottomless sea of shame and despair.

I remember when I first hopped onto the merry-go-round called the Ferocious Foursome in high school. I decided throwing up would be the perfect fix to a binge. I tried, but was unable able to accomplish the mighty feat. So I tried again, and instantly remembered why I hated getting sick.

At first I felt mad at myself for not being able to purge. At the time I didn't know that 18–20% of people with eating disorders would die within twenty years. I thought purging was the new magic weight-loss answer at the time. I had no idea that years later statistics would flood in about the life-threatening health concerns associated with bulimia. Many would end up accidentally killing themselves due to the horrific damage on their bodies. Bulimia would eat up the lives of many girls and women, leaving behind families in shock and lakes of tears.

As a purging flunky, I skipped level three of the Ferocious Foursome and went on to the final four. I ended up getting addicted to exercise for a few years. Maybe you are wondering how anyone could possibly get addicted to exercise. The biggest reason is that endorphins are produced. Endorphins are similar to opiates and provide a natural high. Another definition describes endorphins as a morphine-like substances originating from within the body. The endorphins, combined with the payoff of looking and feeling superb, attract people into exercising more and more. If you think of over-exercising in those terms, you may begin to understand a person can develop an addiction to exercise.

Another stop on the Ferocious Foursome is that of bulimia. Interestingly enough, bulimia can emerge after a young woman's boyfriend breaks up with her. She begins to recklessly compare herself with other young women, and starts to believe it was all about her size. Comparing and coveting are beasts. No wonder God commanded us not to go there. He knows that comparing and coveting poisons our hearts. Even so, we have all driven in the fast lane of Coveting Road, probably more often than we think. The type of coveting I am referring to is when you see a beautiful, thin woman and you really wish you had her tall, lean body. Part of you believes this would give you the perfect life. The problem is that because we live in a fallen world, there is no perfect life this side of heaven. Not even Skinnihood.

The "stinking thinking" (this is a twelve-step phrase) that *if only I were skinny, then he would not have left me* gets programmed into her heart. She then kicks her dieting into high gear, but later on blows her diet. So she resorts to purging or over-exercising.

Once the stinking thinking takes root in her heart, she feels if she was thinner, then she could have kept her boyfriend. Sometimes the guys throw darts of violent words about their girlfriends' bodies, but even if they don't, the girls are often spurred into bulimia. The hundreds of thousands of messages in the media that endlessly echo "to be thin is to be beautiful, and to be beautiful is almost everything" shoot darts into her heart until it bleeds tears. Then she launches into the magical thinking that if she were thin, her life would be practically perfect.

Since they cannot stay on the diet wagon forever, dieters quickly grasp the idea that they can throw up their food and get away with it. Bulimia is profoundly more damaging than once thought. Those of us who were "too sissy" to purge finally realized it was a blessing in disguise. My heart cries oceans of tears for those who are entangled with the beast of bulimia. It is a wolf in sheep's clothing, as it seems so innocent in the beginning. Yet there is always hope! If you struggle with an eating disorder of any type, including anorexia, bulimia, over-exercising, or compulsive overeating, please go to the Web site resources at the beginning of this book. Explore the listings and get professional help. Don't let the Body Image Bandit lie to you again and tell you that you can't be freed.

During the over-exercising period of my life I was going through an extremely difficult experience. I left an abusive marriage and moved 1800 miles away from my ex-husband and back home to the Northwest. I felt as though my life began again. I ended up exactly where I knew I would never end up: living in my parents' daylight basement. I escaped my abusive ex-husband with nothing but my car, some clothes, and various sentimental things I shoved into the trunk before driving away with my parents.

I used exercise as a drug at that time of my life. It was the way I made myself feel better. I spent three to four hours almost every day at the gym. The swimming pool, weight room, and cardio machines were my best friends. Working out was also a way to pass the time and put depression on hold for two or three hours after I left. Also, I thought if I became strong enough physically, I could protect myself from abusive men. Then someone told me you do that with your head and not your body, which made a lot of sense.

I always knew I would never get divorced. So the depression that had started during the marriage grew into a big tangled ball of guilt. The shame and despair

I felt at the time was so dark, I considered suicide. But somehow I kept going. Through that period of time, I kept running into people who told me about a church about twenty miles from home.

I had concluded at the time that God ruined my life with a bad marriage and bad health because I had ankylosing spondylitis and later developed SLE lupus. I was ticked off at God. So I groaned inside when people invited me to church. The woman who cut my hair told me about it first. Then, while substitute teaching in public schools, various teachers told me about it. That was odd because the church was located about thirty miles from the schools I taught in. I tried not to be rude, but wished the wacky church people would go away and leave me alone.

Eventually I decided to visit the church to get the people off my back. I knew God had nothing to offer me, and we were not on speaking terms, in my opinion. The plan was to go to the church, sit in the back, and bolt out so a flock of church ladies didn't rush at me, badgering me or inviting me to come back. Or – worse case scenarios – try to get my phone number or pray for me. I needed an escape route! There's nothing like being tackled with love by a smiling flock of chatting church ladies.

The day I mustered up the courage to walk into the church, an older gentleman named Chuck greeted me. He nonchalantly mentioned they had classes for single, divorced, and married people. I whispered to him, "I'm divorced" and half way thought he would kick me out. I felt like I had a big "D" tattooed on my forehead that announced to the world I was divorced. For some reason I expected him to pass out when I said the "D" word, but it rolled off his lips just as if he had said the word "tree" or "dessert." There was no tone of shame whatsoever in Chuck's voice, which was a gift because I already had cloaked myself in a dark robe of shame.

Since I had arrived too early for the church service, I decided to attend a class instead of going home because Chuck was too nice of an elderly gentleman for me to jet out. Ugh. Now I would have to suffer through not only a boring, stupid church service, but a boring, stupid Sunday school class as well, I thought. I wished I would have stayed home and pumped more iron.

Chuck walked me to the divorce recovery class. I discovered I couldn't sit in the back because the chairs formed a circle. *Oh no! I'm doomed.*

As I sit writing this twenty years later, I am searching for words to describe how that day turned my life from a bleak, chaotic mess into a colorful quilt of hope. Of course this side of heaven, life can't be perfect because we live in a tainted world. Jesus promised we would have trouble, although you don't see that printed in the pretty little books about God's promises. He also promised he would never leave us or forsake us. John 16:33 says, "Here on earth you will have many trials and sorrows. But take heart, I have overcome the world."

In the divorce recovery class I learned life is not about going through the motions, going to work, coming home, working out, and getting up the next day to do it all over again. Nor is it about getting ahead, keeping up with the Jones', or having a lot of toys so you can have fun.

What I learned on that prominent day was that life is about relationships. I learned Jesus paid all my debts on the cross, and I was created to have a life-changing relationship with him. He is available to talk with me and He speaks to me through the Bible. Most importantly, I learned Jesus is passionately in love with me, and He really has my back, even when it doesn't seem like it. He does have guidelines for me

– not to zap my fun, like I used to think. But He has standards for me so I don't get hurt. I never understood that until I earned my Ph.D. from the School of Hard Knocks.

I had always thought life was about being "successful" in the eyes of the world, which meant having a rewarding career, a beautiful home, and the so-called "good life." Years later, however, I discovered that people who live in the wealthy suburbs also have the highest rates of depression and suicide in America. The Amish have the lowest rates, and although they have their own problems, they may have a lot to teach the rest of us.

Jesus chased after me passionately and He is my biggest cheerleader. I fell wildly in love with Him and studied his Word with every minute I could spare after that day, but still could not get enough. Finally I decided to go to seminary to take a crash course of Bible packed into a nine month school year. To this day, I continue on my journey of walking with Jesus.

One day as I was walking out the door to go to the gym, a verse came to mind. The verse is 1 Samuel 16: 7, "Man looks at outward appearance, but God looks at the heart." Other verses that danced in my head that day included the passage in Matthew 6:19–20 which states, "Stop storing up treasure for yourselves on earth, where moths and rust destroy and where thieves break in and steal, but keep on storing up for yourselves treasures in heaven, where moths and rust do not destroy and where thieves do not break in and steal."

Gradually I ran away from the Ferocious Foursome. My life took on new meaning as I entered into a relationship with Jesus and discovered He is much more interested in how well I love than how I look. He is much more concerned with my heart than the size of clothes I wear or the size of my tooshie. As I let that seep into my skin and inhabit my tattered heart, my perspective changed. Instead of letting societal standards of exterior beauty cut me into shreds, I decided to start looking at myself more the way God looks at me. Of course living in a fallen world means the Bandit throws photo shopped, air-brushed beauty standards in my face throughout the day, and so I won't be fully released from all the issues until I get to Heaven. I still struggle with these issues, but deep down I know my value comes from my heart and not the size of my bottom. But even so,

I feel much better about the way God has created me after immersing myself in Scripture.

The best ammunition for the bullets shot at us by the Beauty Image Bandit, who is the enemy, is to be saturated in the Word of God. Memorizing Scripture keeps my ammunition belt full for those times when the Bandit pellets me with images that make me feel like crumbs instead of a seven course meal. That keeps me on target so I don't obsess over the size of my jeans. I kissed the quest for Skinnihood goodbye.

Chapter 4

Faces and Masks

Pacific Ocean air streamed through my hair as I pedaled along the bike path from Ojai toward Ventura in southern California, near the Ventura County line the Beach Boys sang about. Rolling green hills greeted me as massive, two-hundred-year-old oak trees seemed to assure me I would be okay. Their towering presence and steadfast trunks reminded me they had weathered sleet, hail, earthquakes, and windstorms. I needed the reassurance at the time, as my life felt out of control due to some difficult issues.

A dog walked calmly with its owner off leash about a hundred feet ahead. Unfortunately, he freaked as I approached him, zigzagging all over the path. I hit my brakes, but it was too late. The sudden braking catapulted me over the handlebars. I slid along the asphalt; face first, until I came to a heap. I saw little stars around my head like they show in cartoons.

The dog's owner asked if he could drive me to the hospital in his truck, but my brain couldn't think straight due to the head injury. The only thought I had was, "Never get in a car with a stranger," so I refused his offer. I believe the concussion affected my thinking because looking back, I am surprised I didn't accept the ride. I rode home, and blood dripped down my shirt from the wound.

When I entered the doctor's office, the nurse led me back immediately. The doctor carefully scrubbed the asphalt out of my chin and cheek with a soft plastic brush. After stitching my face, he told me I would probably need skin grafts in the future.

Before leaving the clinic, I decided to use the restroom. As I opened the door, a mirror flashed a monster-like person looking back at me. I startled and moved back about six inches in disbelief. "Oh no," I said to myself. Even though the doctor had bandaged the wound, scrapes and scratches beat up the left side of my face. But I convinced myself it was probably not nearly as bad as I thought. The doctor had left the scrapes uncovered so they could heal. I decided it was probably not nearly as daunting as it seemed, sort of like when you're overcritical of a picture of yourself.

After using the restroom and washing my hands (very carefully, as they were badly scraped from trying to brace myself), I opened the door and walked out. People in the waiting room gawked at me.

We stopped to fill some prescriptions, and I waited in the car with the window rolled down. People driving into the parking lot did double takes and stared. Later we drove to a movie rental place where the same thing happened. This made me feel like a monster. I thought people taught their children not to stare at disfigured people. But apparently not everyone received the lesson. Or else the wounds shocked people and they couldn't control their gut reactions. I felt like Frankenstein's long-lost cousin.

My face turned different colors throughout the healing process from the bruising and scabbing. I avoided leaving the house as much as possible. I taught school on a year-round schedule at the time, and had November off. I expected my face to heal completely by the first week of December.

Sometimes I thought about how disfigured people must feel. Waves of guilt ravaged me as I remembered how I used to saturate myself in magazines and wish I had more prominent cheekbones and larger eyes. Now I would give anything just to look normal.

My first day back at school, the students peppered me with questions. The healing stage was long and arduous. Periodically, tiny pieces of asphalt rose to the surface, just like the doctor said would happen. I wondered if I would ever heal completely, or if I'd need skin grafts. Even a year later the healing process continued. The final stage involved applying a bleaching cream to lighten the red skin tone.

Over twenty years later, the scars are unnoticeable to most people. I see slight discoloration on the left side of my chin, which I could easily cover with scar makeup, but it doesn't bother me. The accident is part of my story, and what makes me who I am. Thankfully, I never needed skin grafts.

The accident scared my parents. My mom asked me to promise I would never ride my bike alone again. I promised but didn't have the courage to get back on a bike for a few years. After moving back to Washington, I decided to give it a try. I asked various women friends and acquaintances to ride with me, since I had promised my mom I wouldn't ride alone. Usually they said yes. But when we sped up they complained, "Oh no! My heart is beating fast!" *You've got to be kidding. That's what it means to work out!* Some said, "Yuck! I'm really sweating!"

One day a year or so later, I told some church friends about my cycling accident, and how I had promised mom that I would never cycle alone. I expressed my discouragement in trying to find a compatible riding partner. They suggested I ask George, an older guy I'd met in the divorce recovery class I attended and they led. I doubted he could keep up with me. I decided to ask him because they said he raced bicycles years ago and still liked to ride.

During that time I worked out a great deal and had lost about twenty pounds due to depression. Because of that, men asked me out right and left, but I wanted nothing to do with them because I knew they were more interested in my body than my heart. Something inside me told me that first of all, I was nowhere near being ready for a relationship. As I learned in the divorce recovery class, getting into a new relationship before two years or so would be like trying to run a marathon with broken legs. But even if the two years had elapsed, I knew these guys would be gone if I gained back the twenty pounds I lost. All they cared about was my packaging.

Even though George and I attended the same

class, we didn't know much about each other. Our age difference meant our paths almost never crossed. Nevertheless, I asked him to go on a twenty mile bike ride, and he said yes. We agreed on a day, time, and place, but the sky started to cloud up with big black clouds, so I called to ask if he would like a rain check.

"Oh no, I'm sure it'll blow over," he said.

We rode on a popular trail in the Seattle area and stopped at a restaurant for lunch. The whole time we pedaled, I learned more about George's story and realized what a wise, fun person he was. About halfway through my French dip, I wondered, *Where have guys like this been all my life?* George was humble, funny, real, and loved Jesus.

George had worked through a lot of issues in counseling and refused to wear a mask. Most people are so terrified of rejection and abandonment they stay behind a mask or façade most of the time. They project not who they really are, but the person they think others want them to be so they will be liked. They hide behind wealth, or perceived wealth, achievements, phoniness, and they are committed to wearing a mask and to not letting people know who they really are. After all, if people knew the real person, would they like him or her, or leave?

When we zone in on making everyone like us, we forget Jesus was completely real and fully present. By this, I mean he said what he meant and meant what he said. We are easily pulled into a storm of untruth that pictures Jesus as a sugary sweet man/God who was always Mr. Nice. But we cannot forget he often called people on their issues, which is part of the recipe of true love. Jesus was not a doormat or a puppet, but he always said what he meant and meant what he said. In our attempts to get people to like us, we construct and put on a mask that only gets thicker with each misrepresentation.

George had learned through the School of Hard Knocks to take off the mask and deal with the issues in his heart. He exhibited the courage to reveal his true self – his thoughts, feelings, mistakes, and struggles. When was the last time I had heard someone take such a risk? Usually people fear if they disclose their areas of difficulty, they will be abandoned or rejected.

I felt refreshed as he unveiled some of his areas of weakness, layer by layer. He took off his mask and placed it on the table right next to us. "Take it or leave it," yet in a kind-hearted way, the mask-less face seemed to say. "This is the real me."

Since he put himself out there, I gained the courage to do the same, little by little. I also sensed George stayed present in our conversations. In other words, he was not off in his head thinking of what to say next. We can easily fall into the trap of not being present, and to do so is to rob ourselves as well as those we converse with. When we hang out in our heads thinking of other things or what to say next, we are not loving each other well.

Munching on the second half of my French dip, I started thinking something was wrong with me. *Why am I enamored by this man?* I used to joke about people who dated older guys and could never understand why a woman would date a guy six or seven years older, let alone ten. But twenty? Absolutely ridiculous.

We didn't notice during our animated conversation over lunch that the sky had come unglued and dumped more water than we had ever seen—even for Seattle. We had soaked in each other's presence to the point our surroundings faded into oblivion. When we finally came to, we saw cars hydroplaning on ponds that used to be streets. A man in a Cadillac asked if we wanted a ride, and we took him up on it (even though the "don't ride with strangers" record spun in my head).

Throughout the next weeks and months, George occupied a huge percentage of my brain space. Confusion engulfed me as I mulled over our significant age difference. In the meantime, we continued to be involved in the same group activities at church. People began to ask about us as the months went by. Many said we were meant for each other. Each of us always said we were "just friends," and they often laughed or responded, "Oh, right" in disbelief. Most people easily saw that we took to each other like mozzarella cheese on pizza.

I continued to heal from a bruised heart. Although recovery is not a mathematical formula, most professionals say it takes at least two to five years to grieve and recover from a divorce, although the divorce will leave a scar. The prominence of the scar depends on how well you recover from it based on many factors and how committed you are to working through your issues. But of course there is no substitute for time. You cannot press the fast forward button on healing time.

Seasons went by and a few years got away from us. I had learned from the divorce recovery class that once a person is healthy and healed (several years after the divorce), she should date a person for about two years before marrying him. Otherwise she is probably marrying his mask, not the real person behind the facade. The theory behind this is that then you can see each other through all the seasons as well as some difficult life experiences. You will truly know how he handles sadness, anger, rejection, and the ups and downs of everyday life. The real person emerges as the mask grows thinner over time. This is one reason why a whirlwind romance (in which the couple moves in together or marries) is often a red flag. Most abusive relationships start that way.

During the years George and I hung out and shared hopes, dreams, and fears, I decided to go to Multnomah Seminary to take a year-long crash course in Bible with other professionals, which I'd dreamed about since I was eighteen. The school was in Portland, and we wondered if our relationship would weather the distance and time, but George always encouraged me to chase my passions and lasso my dreams. That was another thing about him I found exceptionally attractive.

Driving down Interstate 5 to visit the school, thoughts and prayers spun around in my head as the tires rolled along the asphalt. At one point I prayed, "God, if I get married again, I would love for it to be someone like George." Just as I said the prayer, a Just Married car went by. *Hmmm...interesting.*

I drove several more miles, praying and thinking about many different things. Then I came back to my original prayer: "Lord, if I get married again, I pray that it would be to someone like George." Immediately a different Just Married car passed. It definitely was not the same one as before. *How weird.* I started to wonder if God was telling me something. But I was not a person easily convinced.

Finally I became convinced we were meant to be together. People saw us as a great fit – except my parents freaked out at the relationship due to our age difference. "Cherrie, George is from the Elvis generation," Mom said. And I can't say I blame her. I am sure our age difference occupied a great proportion of her hard drive. She would have been surprised to know I had written lists of what the age difference would mean if we ever married. The probability of having to take care of him in Depends, with Alzheimer's, and not having children (or his being an older father to them) all crossed my mind several times per week once we got serious.

Part of me knew we were meant to be together because of the Just Married cars, and the scriptures about marriage that popped up when I happened to think about George. I wanted God to essentially tell me directly I should marry George. Why couldn't he send me an email or put a sticky note on the fridge to tell me what to do? I mean, God created the Grand Canyon and all the beautiful mountains in the world, so how much trouble would it be for him to shoot me one little email or stick a Post-it note on the fridge? Come on, God. Give a little!

After straining my brain to figure out a way for God to show me his plan for our relationship, I decided to pull something really bizarre out of the air. Let me tell you, I picked something really out there, and I don't know how I came up with it. I didn't know scripture very well at the time, and so you could say that in some respects I tested God. Since Scripture says we are not to test God except in terms of tithing (Malachi 3:10), I now believe I went too far. So I want to emphasize I do not recommend trying this because it has no solid spiritual basis.

This is where things got really weird. For some reason - I don't remember how - I decided I would tell God: "If you really want George and I to get married, please show me the date we are supposed to get married in orange paint. Not just some little tiny writing that I can barely see, but bright orange paint that is mega obvious." (As I already said, I think I definitely took things too far at the time, but that is where I was in my knowledge of scripture at the time. I know that putting out fleece, so to speak, like Gideon did is a good idea, but in my heart of hearts this now feels like testing God because God had already spoken to me through circumstances, the Bible, and other believers.)

What George didn't know at the time was my rheumatologist had told me having children would be very difficult with my severe case of ankylosing spondylitis. He also had said that if I had a boy, he would have a higher chance of getting AS, which is an incredibly painful disease. So I had pretty much written off the possibility of having children because it didn't seem fair for me to take that kind of risk. I know that many people feel differently, but that is what felt right for me in my situation.

Since George and I had agreed to be open about issues as they came up, I decided to tell him about mom's comment he was from the Elvis generation. Even though I didn't want to hurt his feelings, I thought he should know. He was on the church worship team at the time, and he immediately broke into singing Elvis's "Hound Dog." Then he told me if we ever got married, he would wear a white Elvis bell-bottomed pantsuit. We laughed so hard, we could barely breathe.

I noticed we could have fun even without going somewhere fancy. In fact, we both had empty pockets at the time and often hung out at cafés drinking cheap coffee. My ex and I had often spent a great deal of money going to spendy activities and places so we could have fun. To this day, I am convinced that if you can drink cheap, yucky coffee with someone and you really have a great time anyway, that is a good test.

Without all the fluff involved in the dating process, going to elegant places, spending big bucks, you can get much closer to the real person behind the mask.

During Christmas break my dad took me to my rheumatologist to receive cortisone injections in my feet as a last resort. I chickened out for a week or so, but a week of lying on the couch and crawling to the restroom was enough. I finally toughed it out and got the injections, which helped somewhat. My rheumatologist also put me on a low dose of chemotherapy, which meant that I would have to go back to Seattle for check-ups periodically once I went back to Portland.

I called my professor to explain my situation. I said it was the best year of my life thus far, but I didn't think I could continue because my body couldn't handle the stress.

Dr. Bruce Fong, my amazing professor, recommended cutting down my work load by cutting my course load in half. I realized it would mean I would not get the Bible Certificate at the end of the year, but decided the Multnomah program, for me was more about the experience than the certificate.

When the graduate students reconvened in January, I cut my course load in half and felt lighter, as though I could flit around like a butterfly and enjoy life once again. In fact, I had a superb time and still enjoyed the social life with other grad students.

In February I had an appointment in Seattle for the checkup with my rheumatologist. During the long drive, I prayed about my relationship with George, and asked God why he had not given me the "orange paint sign" I had asked for. I admit I whined a lot about the situation and finally decided to tell

God, "Okay, if you don't want George and I to get married, please give me wisdom to find the right words to break up with him." I sighed and realized the cars slowing down to about ten miles per hour on Interstate 5 North, which was exceptionally rare.

I had to use the restroom badly, but a huge flood had ravaged the area, making it difficult to move, let alone get over to the right so I could exit. Water sat in the streets of Kamala and my bladder felt as full as the streets. "God," I prayed, "please help me to find a restroom, and also give me just the right words since you haven't given me the orange paint sign—"

"*No way!*" I said aloud to nobody. My heart felt as though it was on overload. A car that had bit the dust sat on the shoulder of the road waiting to be towed. I would not have noticed if traffic had not been crawling along at the pace of a drunken squirrel. In the rear window of the car, bright orange paint which took up almost the entire window said, 2-16.

A few days ago George and I celebrated our seventeenth wedding anniversary (although we did not marry in February but in May, because our church told us they would not marry people on Sundays due to the packed schedule). I never in my wildest dreams thought marriage could be so joyous. My husband tells me these have been the best years of his life, and I tell him the same thing. Of course no marriage is perfect, and all marriages have some valleys. But I feel incredibly blessed that the valleys have been short, and rare.

I am amazed my emotionally and physically painful cycling accident led to a series of events which provided me with the opportunity to get to know George. I remember watching an episode of Extreme Makeover Home Edition, and a woman thanked God for the rain that had caused the flood that led to her house getting beautifully remodeled. Although the rain and flooding caused misery and pain at the time, it led to beauty. And now I say, "Thank you, Lord, for the bicycle accident, which led to my getting to know the wonderful man who is now my husband."

Chapter 5

Birthdays

You Can't Live with 'Em, and You Can't Live Without 'Em –Or Can You?

If you have the number for the birthday police, I need it. Last February I received a postcard in the mail from my gynecologist letting me know my next Pap smear was due on my birthday. Of course, I had the option of going in a few weeks early so my birthday would be free of paraphernalia down in my South America. Bless her little heart for giving me the option of choosing another week.

Since my driver's license and my professional license also expire on my birthday, I do have other options for my special day. Either way, I was left with three unforgettable choices for celebrating my birthday:

1. Get a Pap smear

2. Renew my driver's license

3. Renew my professional license

What kind of a joke is this? We need birthday police to make sure that nothing expires on our birthdays. What's wrong with having licenses and pap smears expire on our half birthday? That would mean on August 18, half way between my last and next birthday, my licenses and Pap smear would expire. I could deal with that.

Speaking of birthdays, I plan to celebrate mine until I reach the age my teeth, hearing, and memory are all gone. I want to milk my birthday for all it's worth. Presents, parties, special dinners, and cards – bring them on! Okay, I realize I may not feel this way in the future, but as of right now, it sounds like a good deal.

A few weeks ago I had lunch with a friend in her early thirties. The conversation turned to birthdays and age. She commented on a TV commercial where a lady was talking critically about parentheses lines around her mouth. This ad angered my friend. She told me faces were meant for lines, and how they define us and make us beautiful in unique ways.

I told her to let me know if she feels the same

way in the next fifteen years. I sincerely hope she does.

My husband tells me as the sun begins to set on his life, people don't seek him out as much as they used to. This saddens both of us because he has much wisdom and experience to offer. And the cherry on top is his wonderful sense of humor. But because people brush him off as *older* or a senior citizen, they exclude him. He is physically active, and many of the thirty-something guys he works construction with have said they hope to be in such great shape when they are his age. He is definitely a chip off the old block. His mother recently celebrated her 94th birthday, and up until a few years ago, she personified strength and dignity.

"Age is just a number," is a line you've probably heard many times. I know I have. My mother-in-law used to say that phrase a lot. Then she said the same thing about five seconds later, and again five seconds later, and yet again five seconds later. But I do give her a lot of credit because in many ways she was an amazing woman. If I make it even to my eighties, I may not even know my name. You may see me running around on the freeway with my Hello Kitty pajamas on. (I'm addicted to Hello Kitty. What can I say?!) If you see me there, please take me back to where I belong.

A few years ago my husband showed up unexpectedly at my friend's house where I was visiting. "It's Mama," he said. He looked at the floor, a tear sliding down his cheek. "She broke her hip."

I threw on my jacket and we raced to the hospital. I couldn't picture Dorothy with a broken hip. She seemed as though she would live forever, and that she had always existed. Mama is an oak tree that grows stronger and statelier under the pressures of time. How could she have broken her hip? That was reserved for elderly people, and Mama didn't qualify, even at 88. After my mother-in-law said, "Age is just a number," she added, "It's what you do with your life that counts."

Images of my beloved mother-in-law filled my head as we drove to the hospital. I pictured her mixing and pouring concrete with me a few years ago to secure a birdhouse in her mini Garden of Eden. Scenes of many people who idolized Mama flashed in my mind, most of them gathered around the fireplace in her den. Mama's place was like Saturday morning at Starbucks, with friends passing through, knowing they can't stay forever although they would like to.

Her home felt simple but cozy, with a glowing wood fireplace and red shag carpeting from the seventies, a place that made my soul smile. On the dark paneled wall of her den hung a Volunteer of the Year award. I pictured her gnarled fingers sorting vegetables for the food bank she ran out of her garage every Friday. Her epitaph could have read, "Throwing away food is a sin." Guilt ravages me on those rare days I muster the courage to clean out my refrigerator and find fossilized food that would test the skills of the finest hazmat team.

After her fall, Mama spent a few days recuperating from surgery in the hospital until her Medicare benefits ran out and she was transferred to a nursing home. Like many people, she had always insisted she would never go to a nursing home, and we dreaded how the transfer would affect her. She had expected to be in the hospital for her entire recovery, and then to go directly home. George and I grasped hands tightly as we walked in to visit her the first night at the nursing home. My heart raced as I contemplated what the nursing home stay would do to her. Would she recover, or would depression set in? The hip would heal, but we weren't sure Mama's spry spirit would recover from her stay at the facility.

As we approached the bed, Mama said tearfully, "I never wanted to be in a nursing home." She grabbed George's hand in her own swollen, distorted one that had weathered thousands of hours harvesting sugar beets as a child. "You've got to get me out of here if they don't treat me good."

George promised he would. As he said this, I felt the room fill with love and recalled how she said on his birthday every year, "George, we were so happy when you were born. We wanted a son so much." Although they had their spats, George and Mama maintained a deep connection.

As we left Mama's room, I thought about a day she and I got stuck in the monstrous Seattle traffic while shopping for her gingerbread house supplies. She had asked me, "Where is everybody going, and why are they in such a hurry?" She wrinkled her forehead and scrutinized me. "They won't be home for dinner, and in the long run that's gonna cause them a whole heap of trouble. Ya know, a lot of people lose their families 'cause they're not home for dinner enough."

I shivered with guilt thinking about how I had nothing ready for dinner. If I hadn't heard her friends tell me she enjoyed me, I would have been ashamed. "They're so busy making more money so they can have bigger, fancier houses. They never sit down with the families to have dinner. Next thing ya know, they lose their families."

We agreed on many things, and that was one of them. Mama's wisdom surpasses many whose names are buried in piles of initials for all the degrees they've earned, even though she had to quit school after seventh grade to work on the farm. By age eleven, she was taking care of her younger siblings and driving the horse and buggy into town to pick up staples. Those priorities didn't leave time for school.

The second day I visited Mama, I flung open the doors of the nursing home and whiffs of popcorn titillated my nostrils. A fire engine red, old-fashioned popcorn maker made the reception area smell like a movie theatre. Walking down the hall, I marveled at the gorgeous window treatments and plush carpeting. Wallpaper adorned the walls, and I halfway expected Martha Stewart to poke her head out of one of the rooms with a freshly baked batch of cookies. I opened Mama's room and took in the cheery pale yellow décor with border print and upbeat framed art. Maybe George and I could move in here, I thought.

Mama regained her Mama-ness overnight. Her

pink cheeks reflected long days spent tending her glorious garden, complete with a pond, small waterfall, a creek, and several bridges. A smile punctuated her sentences. "I'll be out of here in no time," she said. "Like my friends who had this operation told me, I'll work really hard, so I'll go home soon. Marie told me, 'If they tell ya to do ten exercises, do twelve.'" I thought her recovery would take longer, but reminded myself this was not the average person. This was Mama, and nobody dare underestimate Mama.

The next day I began the first of many scavenger hunts to find my mother-in-law. Usually nobody could help me because she zipped around like the Energizer bunny on wheels. I found her in a resident council meeting, a concert, physical therapy, the gym, the beauty shop, and hanging out with new friends. They were laughing so hard, I could feel the walls vibrate. One day they went to inner-city Seattle to distribute blankets to the homeless.

I told my friends about Mama's great attitude in the nursing home, and they figured she liked the facility and would enjoy living there. Evidently they didn't understand she didn't like it, but Mama usually made the best out of her circumstances. When life gave her lemons, she makes lemon meringue pie and threw a party. She didn't want to be there because her life sprung up out of her home, where her food bank and flower garden became extensions of her essence. But since she had to be in a nursing home, she decided to make the most of it. She took advantage of every activity and made some great new friends.

One day Mama called me on the phone. "Hey, bring in Custer." Custer is our only child—a squirrelly, spoiled golden retriever. I pictured Custer licking the fragile folks on the lips. I cringed at the idea of bringing her in, and told Mama it wouldn't work.

"They've got dogs all over the place here," she said. "Bring her on down."

What she said was true. I remembered seeing several well-trained, calm dogs that sat sweetly like dog-angels. But no out-of-control, hyperactive ones like Custer. I wanted to add to Mama's way of creating joy whenever life spat on her, so I had Custer hop in the car, and we drove to the nursing home. As soon as I pulled into the parking lot, I spotted Mama waiting outside.

"HEY, CUSTER!" Mama yelled across the parking

lot in a voice heard clear to Montana. I gripped the leash tightly as Custer bounced across the parking lot to lick her favorite person on the lips, restraining her just as she tried to pretend she was a lap dog and land her 55-pound body onto Mama's wheelchair.

"C'mon. Let's go inside so everybody can meet you guys," said Mama, rolling her wheel chair toward the entrance.

As soon as we opened the door, Custer's nose and eyes fixated on the enormous popcorn maker. Entranced, she forgot she came to visit her grandma. Mama sprinted her wheelchair across the room to get the spoiled retriever a heaping bag of popcorn. And of course Custer inhaled the salty treat like she hadn't eaten in months. "Dontcha ever feed this dog?" she asked, as she gave me a look out of the corner of her eye. Custer licked Mama's fingers just before Mama reached in to grab a handful of popcorn for herself. "Dog's saliva is healing," she said. Several residents rallied around and petted Custer, who ate the attention up like a trip to the dog park.

Often when I went to visit, Mama sweated it out in the gym. At first it was hard to believe my 88-year-old mother-in-law had transformed from a short, blue-eyed, white-haired grandma into a hot exercise babe. Her round little German frame was like steel from pumping iron.

The day I picked Mama up to drive her home, she sported a new peach-colored workout suit a neighbor had brought her. I helped her climb into the car and put the walker in the back. After climbing into the driver's seat, she rolled down the window to say good-bye to the entourage that had gathered to wish her well. "I'll be back to help you guys take care of the old people," she told the social services director, once again removing herself from the definition of old people. "I know you're really busy, and I love to volunteer, so I guess I'll see ya again as soon as I get better—probably in a month or so. After all, age is just a number. It's what you do with your life that counts."

As I pulled out of the parking space, my heart filled with a longing to grow as wise as Mama.

While pondering some of the older people I know, a special man popped on the screen of my mind's eye. Each of the past five years I have written a Christmas letter to friends and family. Clayton starred in the one I wrote last year. Due to email and Facebook, the people my husband and I care most about already know what's going on in our lives, so I decided to do something different with our annual Christmas tidings. I tell stories and encourage people to fix their eyes on the real Christmas star. This is the version from last year, which featured a wise old gentleman:

> Dear Friends and Family:
>
> This can't be happening, I told myself. Clayton seemed to have been around forever. Not only that, but part of me hoped and prayed that he would live forever. You could almost drown in his ocean blue eyes, and his smile would knock you to the ground if you weren't braced. Clayton seemed as stable as Christmas itself.
>
> Rumor had it that the elderly gem of a gentleman had deeper pockets than Santa, and that he dipped into them whenever his heart sang a sad song for someone. That turned out to be quite often. Clayton once helped a family buy a home, and he bought cars for others in need. Sometimes I

wondered if he was too generous with his money, but I guess that was his own business. I used to worry that people would take advantage of Clayton's humongous heart, which probably filled most of his body.

Clayton's heart danced to a distinctly different drum beat – the drum beat of love. His passion was serving, and he threw his soul into the eight private food banks he ran. Dawn was still asleep when Clayton crawled out of bed, ate breakfast, and drove his older Mercedes to Costco, Albertsons, QFC and other local stores to pick up day-old food to drive to his beloved food banks. One summer George asked him if he was going on vacation, and he responded, "Who would pick up the food?" Then he dashed off in his sleigh – I mean his Mercedes, and gallivanted off to his next stop.

Maintaining eight food banks kept Clayton busy, but he still found several hours each week to transport people with MS and cancer to their medical appointments. He also volunteered in his church.

Shortly after 9/11, I asked Clayton, "Do you ever worry?" He smiled, answered, "No," and pointed to heaven. I breathed a sigh of relief as I remembered that even when it doesn't seem like it, God is in control. And in the end, the good guys and gals always win. The deal is that sometimes we have to wait.

One year Clayton decided he wanted chicken and dumplings for his birthday dinner and asked my mother-in-law, Dorothy, to cook for him. I used to tease her, saying they could get married in her back yard that exploded blossoms and beauty. Her daughters told her that all of us could be bridesmaids. She turned redder than Santa's suit and insisted they were just friends. But I often saw heart-shaped sparks in Clayton's eyes when he delivered food to Dorothy's garage, which housed one of the food banks.

I don't have many heroes, but Clayton was certainly at the top of the short list. So the summer before last, when a friend called to say that Clayton had died in a car accident, I stopped breathing for a few seconds. I couldn't believe that the stop button was pushed on Clayton's life. The accident happened on a major road in front of a QFC grocery store in Kirkland, and he died upon impact. Food rained all over 124th Street. Costco poppy seed muffins, spinach, lettuce, oranges, potatoes, and chocolate cake with creamy frosting decorated 124th Street like snowflakes falling at Christmas. Clayton had planned on zipping in to pick up a woman to drive her to cancer treatment before delivering the food to his next stop. But of course he never made it because he made a detour to heaven.

We pray you will embrace the true

meaning of Christmas. And remember that Clayton was right. We have nothing to worry about because God has given us a perfect gift. The paradox is that it was not wrapped in a Nordstrom box and placed under a tree. It was actually a baby man-God wrapped in swaddling cloth and placed in a manger. That is truly the greatest gift of all. May you be a gift to your friends and family this Christmas and forever, just as Clayton was a gift to all who knew him. God bless,

George and Cherrie

Scripture teaches us that age brings forth wisdom. Gray hair is to be esteemed, the Bible says, but in our society we pluck them out and dread the aging process. The media teaches us thin and tall is good, and wrinkles and gray hair are bad. Plastic surgery is a booming business. Flocks of women and men walk through the doors of plastic surgeons every day in the hopes of erasing years from their physiques. They believe if they are younger looking good things will happen to them. They fight old age and death with a syringe full of solution they hope will turn back the hands of Father Time.

I noticed just the other day, for the first time, my skin has lost its elasticity and now consists of a jillion mini wrinkles sitting shoulder to shoulder. No kidding, it seems like this wrinkle farm appeared overnight. Although I entertain the idea it happened gradually and I didn't notice until last week. Suddenly I began to think of what caused it and what I could do to rectify the problem. Admittedly, I am sad my creases feel like a *problem* I have to *fix.*

I am a few corners past fifty, so maybe this new freak-out mode will be something I fight from here on out. (That is certainly an unpleasant thought.) I think the all-over mini-wrinkled skin issue, in my case, is the shadows of sun-drenched skin. Living on Maui, in southern California, and Arizona, I let sneaky sun rays steal the elasticity from my skin. Although I wore sunscreen, my skin was burned for almost the entire two years I lived on Maui. Friends came to visit and we'd warn them to wear sunscreen, but they'd say they didn't need much. After a couple of days in the tropical sun, they spent their time soaking several hours a day in a bathtub full of cold water because of their third degree burns.

In some cultures, such as the Japanese, aging is considered the grand gateway to the doors of wisdom and respect. Sadly, in our culture, aging is considered the dark tunnel to disrespect. Recently I had my hair highlighted and cut by my friend Sophia, who is originally from Thailand. She reminded me that in many other countries, such as her own, the elderly are treated as though they are the finest gems in the trunk. In fact, the younger people literally bow to their elders. I reminded Sophia since she is two years younger than me, she should bow to me and respect me. Thankfully, she knew I was kidding. I greatly enjoy my hair appointments because we share stories and laugh so hard I almost cry.

On the way home from the salon, I wondered what would happen if each elderly person moving into assisted living, memory care, or an adult family home came with a heartfelt letter telling their stories. The positive events, activities, and personality traits highlighted would offer a window to the person's heart. This way the caregivers would recognize the person being admitted has a rich history, passions, likes and dislikes. Then the caretakers would know who this person was when he or she were younger, and be reminded that they, too, will one day grow old. Ideally, the letter would be required reading of everyone in the facility and would cause love to flow through the hearts of the caregivers and warm the residents. For my mother-in-law, for example, the letter would go something like this:

Dear Caregiver:

I would like to introduce you to Dorothy, my mother-in-law, age 94. Her brothers and sisters call her the Grand Marshall because she was the oldest of eight children and used to take charge. Her father died when she was 11, and although she always had many responsibilities, she suddenly became the primary breadwinner for the family. Her swollen, gnarled hands attest to the many years she spent picking sugar beets. She also had to drive the horse and buggy to town to get supplies for the family – all at the ripe old age of 11. Dorothy, or Dot, as some called her, grew up in the Midwest.

She moved to Kirkland in her mid-sixties and cared for her ill husband for seventeen years. Her husband suffered from Parkinson's, Alzheimer's, and depression. Although Dorothy owned a simple, three-bedroom home, her backyard looked and smelled like a mini Garden of Eden. A natural creek ran through the property and George Jr. built a pond, waterfall, and several bridges in the little Eden. Dot planted flowers, bushes, and trees to create a glorious glimpse of paradise. She played an active role in two garden clubs.

In her senior years, Dorothy operated a private food bank out of her garage. Her good friend, Clayton, spent hours each day picking up day-old food from local stores and distributing it to eight private food banks. The delivery, organization, and running of the food bank gave Dorothy and Clayton great joy. Growing up in the Great Depression, they both felt strongly that throwing away food was a sin. At the age of 85, Dorothy received the Volunteer of the Year award from the city of Kirkland, presented by the Mayor, whom Dot knew personally.

Thank you for taking the time to hear the story of this amazing woman, Dorothy. Please treat her as you would like to be treated if you should live a long life.

Sincerely,

Cherrie Michehl

Chapter 6

Real Women Aren't Afraid to Wear Pink:

Getting in Touch with Your Chickness

"MY PINK BAG" boldly adorned the front of a large black handbag I saw in a store window one day. I chuckled and thought of a friend who would rather be sprayed by a skunk than wear pink. She is deeply committed to projecting a tough exterior so nobody can overpower her.

The decision to celebrate or ban pink from a woman's wardrobe often reflects, to some extent, how she feels about being a woman. Some women wish black was the new pink. Others feel pink is their splendor. Every once in a while a woman chooses whether or not to wear the color based solely on how the color looks on her, such as my friend Jill. But that is almost as rare as an ice cream truck parading your neighborhood in December. Usually the decision whether or not to wear pink is caught in a tangled web of a woman's feelings about being female. The color that symbolizes femininity in American culture finds itself invited or expelled from a woman's wardrobe based on her story.

For many women, donning pink would make them feel repressed, stomped on, and fragile. Too "girly." This implies a sense of fragility or powerlessness. Many of them experienced an overwhelming sense of powerlessness they connect with their femininity. All of those feelings play a role in the question of whether or not a woman wears pink. Unless, of course, you are one of the few people that invited or expelled it from your wardrobe based completely on how it looks on you.

Today I am wearing a medium pink velour sweat suit. But before you categorize me into a pink vs. unpink woman, let me explain. I buzzed into the store one day to find an emergency radio for the next big Pacific Northwest storm predicted to knock out our power. But lo and behold, I found the radio quickly and noticed out of the corner of my eye this pink and black camouflage shirt. It was love at first sight. To me, the shirt exudes the phrase, "I am feminine, yet strong." No wonder it is one of my favorite casual tops.

I didn't plan to wear a pink sweat suit with my pink and black camouflage T-shirt while writing this chapter – it just happened that way. I have been told pink is one of my best colors, just like coral and sky blue. That is one reason why I wear pink. When I do, I feel girly. That is why I had to buy the pink and black camouflage shirt when I discovered it in the surplus store.

As I ponder pinkness, I remembered that one of my clients gave me a special gift a few years ago. It was a little plastic toy soldier, which she had painted pink. She told me I represented a woman who was feminine yet strong. I thanked her for it, and will always treasure the little pink painted soldier. After all, who said women should be weak? That is a greatly misunderstood principle because Scripture does not refer to women as weaklings. Yet some people mistakenly believe the Bible encourages women to be delicate, helpless, weak creatures.

Where did I learn to feel feminine and strong – two words which often don't hang out in the same neighborhood? Or maybe a better description would be "feminine, yet capable." We are all mosaics made up of different, unique stories which together create beautiful masterpieces designed by God.

Gender deeply impacts who we are and who we want to become. Our stories also color how we feel about our womanhood or manhood. My own story illustrates these points. Since my parents had two girls and no boys, my sister and I became dad's "boys." He taught us many skills traditionally performed by males in the sixties and seventies. For example, Dad taught us how to change tires. I didn't have a flat until about thirteen years later, and by that time I had forgotten how to do it! The day it happened, I pulled way off to the shoulder, locked my car doors, and started reading the manual in order to click on the refresh button of my memory. (This happened years before cell phones became popular.) As I was reading, a police officer pulled over and approached me with his police dog, whose collar said, "Chico." I chuckled because I remembered an old TV show titled, "Chico and the Man."

The officer asked what I was doing and I said," I'm reading the manual so I can remember how to change a flat tire. My dad taught me when I was sixteen, but obviously it's been a few years."

He laughed and told me he would change the tire for me. I had worn a dress and three-inch heels that day, so I greatly appreciated his kindness. Some women would have declined the offer, but I figured I had nothing to prove, and although I have no problems getting dirty, hiking, and have worked construction, the truth was I did not want to get dirty that evening, especially wearing a dress and heels. And so it came to pass that Chico and the Man changed my flat tire. That was almost twenty years ago, and I haven't had a flat tire since.

Letting Chico and the Man change my tire worked for me because I did not feel I had to prove anything. Some women go to great lengths to prove they are strong, smart, and independent. Those qualities in and of themselves shine, but my heart weeps for those who feel they *have* to prove they are strong due to the powerlessness they felt while growing up. They vowed never to get hurt again and believe an outer layer of toughness will provide the armor they need.

Even though I didn't remember how to change a tire years after dad's instructions, I am grateful I learned how to change tires, hunt, and fish - sort of, because I always had him do the dirty parts, such as dealing with the worm and later gutting the fish!

When I was about nine, Mom and Dad decided

to build a cabin for my grandparents. Dad acquired free lumber from the Bremerton Shipyard, but it was used and full of nails. My sister and I spent many weekends removing the nails from the lumber with crowbars and cat's paws. At the time, I wanted to play instead of help out, but the experience taught me to work hard as well as a bit about the building process. Each weekend we drove our sky blue Jeep pickup from Belfair to Brinnon on the Hood Canal of Washington state. Brinnon was, and still is, spilling over with an abundance of wildlife and the absence of people and traffic. Seals, eagles, deer, starfish, and jellyfish decorate the Canal with magnificent beauty.

Mom taught my sister and me skills which previous generations considered feminine—including sewing, cleaning, and baking. As we grew, both parents encouraged us to participate in activities that interested us - regardless of whether society labeled them as masculine or feminine. Both parents supported our interest in sports as well. Although we had little money, Mom drove us about 25 miles one way to swimming, diving, piano, flute and other lessons. Those skills enriched my life and helped me grow into a well-rounded woman.

My dad insisted my sister and I enroll in strong

math and science courses during high school. I took mostly college prep courses. But my senior year I decided to enroll in an art class instead of physics. After all, I deserved it and wanted to kick back and enjoy my last year. I remember bringing my first project home to show my parents, and Dad looked at it in disgust. He said I needed to withdraw from art class and sign up for physics the next day. My plans swooshed down the drain. At the time I felt cheated when I racked my brain on physics homework while some of my friends played. "Someday it will pay off," Mom and Dad said. *Yeah, whatever.* But I didn't dare tell Dad because he played head coach at our house, and messing with the head coach was like quitting the team.

In these uncertain times, we can travel aimlessly like seaweed in a stormy sea of thoughts and beliefs. How do we know God's heartbeat for women? The women who lived a few generations ago had rigid boxes in which society tried to contain them. Today all the boxes have collapsed, and we live in a Land of Options and Choices. Yet God still greatly values the importance of the family.

Grasping the heart of God's design for woman requires us to delve deeply into Scripture to uncover profound truths about womanhood. I cannot say it any other way: There is no shortcut or instant substitute for taking the time and effort to thoroughly study God's Word. Fortunately, in today's age of choices upon choices, we have many ways to study Scripture. We can buy different versions, the Bible on tape, Kindle, and even on our phones and other devices. Christian book stores and Web sites offer us more study tools to grapple the precepts of God's Word.

This book does not attempt to cover all the significant points about womanhood, but hundreds of works have been written on the topic. One of my favorite resources for studying Scripture, including the subject of femininity, is The Thompson Chain-Reference Study Bible, which contains a marvelous, comprehensive cross reference system. Most of the verses under each category are printed under the subject matter, which makes it easy to study.

Proverbs 31 glitters with jewels of scripture on womanhood. If you've never read it, I encourage you to do so. In the original Hebrew, the proverb consisted of an acrostic using the first 22 letters of the Hebrew alphabet. The bountiful proverb explains the essence of a woman of excellence. Many Bible studies center on the passage as a close-up look at the characteristics of a capable woman. Even so, the passage is not widely understood. Somehow distortion has seeped into its interpretation, creating the false sense that a God-fearing woman is frail.

While studying Proverbs 31 one year, I noticed the writer portrays the woman having strong arms. This shatters the adage that physical weakness is a characteristic that defines the core of a woman. As a matter of fact, the godly woman described in the text exudes strength and is highly valued.

The context of the passage speaks of the woman's dedication to hard work, delegation, and especially about caring for her family and household. The family, in fact, clearly remains at the top of the woman's priories. She also has superb business skills and meets the needs of the poor. Proverbs 31 offers a beautiful collage of true femininity, which includes strength and power as opposed to weakness and powerlessness. I encourage you to read it again as if you were reading it for the first time.

The essence of the Proverbs 31 woman includes a degree of power that does not state, "I am better than a man," but exudes a strength that does not need to prove anything. The woman's heart acts in love as opposed to proving she is tough. She runs her household and business proactively and in no way appears weak or helpless. She carefully plans and does not waste her time.

Today I am reading a book about our second president. The title is *John Adams*, by David McCullough. I enjoyed reading about his wife, Abigail. The women of that era suffered a severe lack of educational opportunities. Their formal schooling stopped at around age seven or eight, and they were strongly discouraged from reading anything other than the Bible. This educational drought created a sense of powerlessness which kept them from painting outside the lines of the tiny boxes society held for women during that time. But fortunately Abigail was allowed to study in her father's library. His library, to Abigail, was like a beautiful, fragrant garden full of life. Fortunately her husband, appreciated her craving for knowledge and encouraged it, which most men frowned upon in her lifetime.

Abigail Adams encompassed many characteristics of a capable wife. She was strong and not weak, independent in many ways, and quite capable. While

John spent a great deal of time away from home while helping to birth this nation, Abigail was in charge of their farm, household, and the education of their children.

Even though Abigail spent hours managing the farm, which was normally done by the man of the house, she was not out to prove anything. Some women today are so wounded they desire to be rock hard and lash out at men in anger. Their goal is to prove they are tough so they aren't wounded further. The hardened exterior – they hope – will serve as a protection from pain. Sometimes this happens when women have been mistreated by others, as in the case of physical, sexual or emotional abuse. Their desire is for people to draw near to them, but the style of relating they developed in childhood is one of abrasion rather than invitation.

God sewed your life quilt with colorful fabrics of your story. Although some of the pieces represent life scenes you'd love to rip out; together they form a splendid work of art. The Lord designed your life story with specific tasks in mind, just as people design quilts for specific purposes. God sewed your quilt for precise reasons. Part of your design includes your femininity.

What would happen if you chose to embrace your femininity, if you haven't already? Don't worry – I'm not talking about spray painting yourself pink. But rather, to study God's design for women in the Bible, and to fully experience your chickness. Your creator pieced your life together with strong, pink thread, to reflect his glory and offer the world a taste of his magnificence. Maybe it's time to rejoice about your chickness. Let's celebrate that we can be strong without sacrificing our femininity. And that amidst the ebb and flow of our culture, you may choose how to live out your true life calling, which includes strong pink thread.

Chapter 7

When Beauty Becomes a Beast

Have you ever wondered what your life would be like if you were drop-dead gorgeous? Perfect. Or close to it, right? Each day would embrace you with a grand gorilla hug. The sun would shine on your back, but not to the point that your armpits would have big ugly pit stains. *Ahhhh ... if only I were exceptionally beautiful.* Sigh. Then you look in the mirror and reality slaps you in the face. *Oh dear. Is this really all I get to work with?* Then you thank the good Lord for the invention of makeup.

I've lived in many places and known a variety of people, including some who are ultra-rich and some who are ultra-beautiful. In fact the exceptionally beautiful bear monumental burdens. That is probably hard for you to understand, unless, of course, you are exceptionally beautiful. In that case, you totally get it.

Back in college, I remember a young woman with beautiful features from head to toe. One day in the cafeteria dinner line I noticed two guys waiting in back of her. They could barely breathe; they were so enamored by her beauty. Finally one of them tapped her on the shoulder, and said, "Your hair is *so* gorgeous." She huffed, looked at them in disgust, and said, "Oh, just mind your own business. I'm so sick of compliments, compliments, compliments, I could just scream." She rolled her eyes, looked at them with disdain, then stomped off to the end of the line to avoid them.

I remember thinking for the first time maybe extraordinary beauty was not the gift I had dreamed it was. Maybe it was not really an easy slide into a homerun lifestyle after all. The same year, I had a new roommate, and she was quite large on top. Riding the elevator down to the lobby of our dorm, another guy friend joined us. His eyes focused on her breasts while talking to her, and she said, "Jerry, if you're gonna have a conversation with me, you need to look at my eyes. My eyes are located quite a bit north of where you are looking." She looked at him with repulsion and his face became the color of Rudolph's nose. The door of the elevator finally opened, and Jerry bolted out.

"Man, I am so tired of that," Sue said. "It makes me feel like a piece of meat or something. I would give anything to be flat-chested or even just normal sized. I am so careful about what I wear, but I can't stop all this sick attention. I never know if they like me for who I really am inside, or for my body. I hate it. I just *hate* it."

We shared stories about developing earlier than the other girls, and how that made us targets of unwanted attention. We both wondered if we would be able to find men who would love us for our hearts and not our bodies. Thankfully, I know my husband loves me for who I am and not my packaging. Of course, nowadays my packaging has some extra padding anyway! But back when I was 17 percent body fat, I wondered how I would ever know if a man liked me for my packaging, or for my heart. I don't know what happened to her, but I hope she found someone who loves her for her heart.

In the days when I was thin, men approached me to ask me out several times per week. I never took them up on it unless I knew them well enough to know they had good hearts. When I had a body men sought out, it scared me. I didn't want that kind of attention. I believe the extra weight I carry now, to some extent, is a boundary of protection to keep the bad out and the good in.

"You are beautiful – inside and outside," my husband says to me. You can tell from my picture I'm not in any way extraordinarily beautiful, so this felt powerful. The first time I heard that, I cried tears of joy. That sentence was as refreshing as a thick piece of juicy watermelon on the hottest day of summer. He often compliments me on different personality characteristics, which I value because it reinforces he pursued my heart and not the packaging. We all long for real relationships in which we can have true intimacy and connect deeply with others.

Recently I interviewed a friend who experienced breast reduction surgery at age twenty-five. Belinda told me as a little girl growing up in a small town, she enjoyed many friendships and remembers being included in neighborhood activities. The girls played basketball, watched movies and attended slumber parties at each other's houses. She fit in well with the group.

Belinda developed breasts two years earlier than the other girls. "It really freaked out my mom and grandma," she said. Not only that, but the girls started to avoid her. When her menstrual cycle started shortly thereafter, Belinda grew even more isolated.

The school system in her town required the students to change schools in the sixth grade, which made her the target of additional crude comments from new school mates. By the seventh grade, she wore a D cup bra size, which she tried to camouflage with baggy shirts. In gym class, the other girls pointed and laughed, provoking Belinda's mom to write a note to change her PE class to last period so she could wait until she arrived home to shower.

In the seventh through ninth grades, Belinda avoided almost everyone. Boys flooded her with calls and attention, often trying to grab her breasts whenever they got the chance. Belinda carried her books close to her chest. But to no avail, the boys pulled the books away.

During high school, Belinda said, "They got rough." One day a group of boys cornered her in an isolated stairwell. They squeezed her breasts, causing horrendous emotional and physical pain. She began to wonder how her life would change with normal sized breasts. She greatly yearned to be known for her heart and not her chest, and to feel cherished and loved because of her personality.

Belinda struggled with dating because, "They always wanted my breasts," she said. However, some of her guy friends and neighbors were respectful of her and treated her with kindness.

While in high school, Belinda started waitressing. As you can imagine, she got a lot of tips even though she always dressed modestly as all women in her family were encouraged to do. During her waitressing years, she was the target of numerous crude comments. One time, her brother overheard one of the comments and jumped out of his booth across the restaurant to tell the guy, (he's 6'3 and weighed 300 pounds) "This is my little sister. If you ever do that again, I will kill you." The guy never bothered Belinda again.

At the age of 17, Belinda wore an EEE size bra cup. "I hated my breasts. They hung down and hurt. I even had to wear a bra at night because of the pain."

Several years later, she married. Eventually she became pregnant and her physician told her she could not breastfeed her children. Hearing the words, tears welled up in her eyes as her soul cried out in pain. The doctor was afraid if she fell asleep while breastfeeding, the newborn would suffocate. This was decades ago, and at the time there was no medication to dry up the milk. So one of her breasts developed an infection, which caused great pain.

Belinda's bank account also suffered extra weight because bras cost three times as much as regular-sized bras.

Eventually she asked her physician about the possibility of breast reduction surgery. He interviewed her to determine if she would be a good candidate. Since her breasts caused her enormous stress, he recommended a reduction. Fortunately, Belinda's insurance paid for the surgery. Backaches, headaches, pocketbook aches, and heartaches. She lost fifteen pounds from the surgery.

About a month after the surgery, Belinda ran into a friend who said, "What happened to your boobs?"

"I got 'em whacked off!" she responded. They both laughed, and Belinda felt a wave of gratitude wash over her. She was no longer treated as a sex object, and she no longer felt the pain in her back and shoulders.

At her ten year class reunion, only a few people recognized Belinda. She had attended school with the same people for twelve years. "But they never saw past the breasts," she said. I felt tears well up in my eyes.

When I asked her if there was anything else she would like to say to women who wish they had large chests, she responded, "It's painful – physically painful and emotionally painful."

Belinda's story shows the truth: The grass is always greener on the other side of the fence. But most of the time, it's Astroturf.

Karen, a lovely African American woman, originally made her appointment for help with depression. Throughout our sessions, her story emerged with tears of sorrow. Her parents wanted her to appear "less ethnic" (their words, not mine) and sent her to plastic surgeons so she would appear more Caucasian.

"They wanted me to keep my hair straightened all the time - but that was only the beginning. They said I would get surgery to make my nose look more Caucasian.

"So I had my first plastic surgery at age thirteen." She showed me pictures of her from before the surgery, in which her nose looked broader. "They also wanted me to be prettier with high cheekbones, and so I had them worked on as well." I saw from the picture her cheekbones were now more defined.

"When I was sixteen, I complained to my parents that boys often commented crudely about my fully developed body, so they let me have a breast reduction for my seventeenth birthday." Each year Karen received more cosmetic surgery. The latest idea her parents had was to bleach out her skin in order to look less African American. Thankfully, she was in her twenties now and told them no. We had been working together for a few months and she realized through and through that her body was her own. She no longer felt powerless about having to give in to their requests.

This story touched a deep place within me because I ached for her to have had a family which loved her for who she was. The message she was not good enough just as God had created her felt like a kick in the stomach.

Karen felt confusion and anger toward her parents and gained the strength to set healthy boundaries with them. This didn't happen overnight, and it was not easy because their love was conditional—based on beauty and achievement. She often felt as though she was a trophy child. She used to look at her perfectionism as a great advantage, but gradually saw it was caused by her desire to attain praise from her parents. Praise was the closest thing to love her home had to offer. Since she couldn't find real, unconditional love, she would settle for praise. And what feeds praise? Usually perfectionism.

Perfectionism is usually based and fueled by shame, and once we began to sort through that, Karen started to evaluate why she continued to raise the bar for herself. She always sought more education, more awards, and to better herself. But she never knew when to stop raising the bar.

Eventually Karen realized God created her to be a human being, not a human doing, and her worth was not in her beauty or her achievements, but that she was a masterpiece – a work of art in God's sight. She now thinks carefully before setting another goal to check if it is about trying to please her parents and get praise as a substitute for their love, or if the goal is more in line with the person God created her to be. With therapy and medication, her depression has lifted and she feels her value as a person, through and through.

"I can't believe what happened this morning,"

Linda said. She had mentioned during the therapy process how she resented her physical beauty. Linda's sleek, dark brown hair and slender, yet athletic frame added to her exotic beauty. People frequently inquired about her ethnicity, although she said she was a mixture of several uniquely distinct ethnicities. "No matter what I do, where I go, or what I wear, guys are always checking me out." Modeling agents propositioned her with a variety of projects, although she never took them up on it. She didn't take the offers because she spent her passion and energy on her life goal of pursuing horticulture.

Linda sighed deeply, tears rolling down her face. "This guy – I have no idea who he is – was taking pictures of me while I was talking with my best friend on the phone. I would have told him to get lost, but Calina and I were deep in our conversation. Where is it gonna end? I would do *anything* to look average. Anything."

She explained how her housemates grew jealous of this attention. "I've tried everything – including wearing ugly clothes – and it just doesn't work." She sighed and a tear echoed her pain. A common theme of her story was the jealousy of other women.

Early in our conversations, I asked Linda, "What

does it mean to you that you are, in many ways, like Esther in the Old Testament?" I knew Linda had an extensive Bible background, and that she was familiar with the story of Esther, who used her beauty for God's glory.

Years ago, I remember thinking that the Old Testament was out of touch and had no impact on my life. Then I attended Multnomah Seminary because I knew almost nothing about the Bible and wanted a thorough knowledge base. So I enrolled in the graduate program where professionals from all over the country and the world gather, live, study, and grow as they eat, live, and breathe the Bible for nine months.

One of my housemates was an attorney who had graduated at the top of her class at the University of Washington School of Law. She told me that the Multnomah grad program was every bit as difficult as law school. Since I was expecting a glorified Vacation Bible School, you can believe I was in for the shock of my life! Even so, attending Multnomah was one of the most beautiful gifts the Lord has ever given me.

Although I was ecstatic to enroll at Multnomah after wanting to do so for over a decade, I remember thinking how I would have to suffer through the Old

Testament. I imagined my friends would have to wake me up if I fell asleep because I was convinced the Old Testament would bore me to no end. Surprisingly, on the first day of class I began to fall in love with the Old Testament. It is powerful and speaks profoundly into our lives as we see ourselves, our stories, our struggles, and our hearts come alive in the vibrant stories of the Old Testament. One of our professors encouraged us to read through the whole Bible every year, and I have tried to do so ever since. This has enabled me to embrace the Old Testament as I see human nature in all its fullness come alive on its pages.

"Hmmm. I guess I've never really thought I had anything in common with Esther," Linda said. She frowned, trying to recall who Esther was and what I was talking about.

"Yeah," I answered. "You and Esther have a lot in common." I refreshed her memory, giving her a brief synopsis of the powerful book of Esther.

God used Esther's beauty and wisdom to save the Jewish race. She used her position for a grand purpose. The verse that best encapsulates her story is Esther 4:14b, which says, "And who knows that you have come to royal position for such a time as this?"

(If you're interested in studying Esther in-depth, I recommend Beth Moore's *Esther: It's Tough Being a Woman*, by Lifeway Press.)

After discussing Esther's story, Linda looked hopeful. "I guess God is sovereign and in control of everything, and he created me this way. I can focus and pray about what good could come out of it instead of concentrate on how to camouflage my looks."

Gradually, Linda began to lean toward her physical beauty instead of turning away from it. She journaled and prayed about how God would use her in the present and the future as she shined along her life path. Although she hasn't abandoned her love for horticulture, she is now able to use her beauty for good. Linda is certainly a budding Esther in the garden of life. She continues to explore her story, strengths, hopes and dreams through the lens of Esther. She knows her life quilt displays meaning in God's plan.

Learning to see herself as an Esther shifted her focus from fear to hope as she celebrates the reasons God chose an Esther pattern for her life quilt.

Linda now chooses to embrace her story and use it for good rather than try to cover her beauty. She feels more at peace now than she has any other time in her life.

Chapter 8

Stalking the Fridge

Substituting Food for Love

"When did you first begin to substitute food for love?" I asked Terri, a twenty-one-year-old college student. She originally came in to work through problems with her boyfriend, but I soon realized the Body Image Bandit was wildly pursuing her. Terri appeared to be about 5'9" and about a size 10.

"I don't really know," she answered, grabbing a tissue from the Kleenex box. "I remember when I had a crush on this guy, Steve, in high school. He was so much fun, and a great guy. And what a dream to look at!" She sighed deeply and looked at the ceiling, almost as if she could see his face. But within a split second, her eyes looked at the floor. She blotted the Kleenex carefully around her eyes, trying not to smear her mascara. "I thought we were getting kinda serious, and we had planned on going to the prom, but he ditched me the week before. We'd been hanging out after school, going to movies, hanging out with friends together, and we even went out to dinner a few times."

"So you were shocked and your heart shattered when he changed his mind," I said. The twenties are my favorite age group to work with. This is the age when people are usually in the process of forming strong patterns in their lives that will deeply impact who they become. Working on their relationships is an integral part of this life passage.

The tears flowed like a tiny waterfall, and her mascara ran despite her attempts to stop it. "He texted me two days before the prom to say he couldn't go after all. He didn't say why, even though I asked him."

"I am so sorry," I said, shaking my head in sorrow and disgust as I heard yet another story of a breakup delivered via text message. If rejection – the Big R – is like a devastating earthquake, then rejection via text is like an earthquake which causes a fire. This turns severe trauma and devastation into a rupture of the heart.

"He ended up at the prom with another girl. I heard about it, then saw the pictures on Facebook. I was so devastated and mad at that jerk! I remember clicking on his Facebook picture, seeing him posed next to this new skinny girl. I really felt like I was gonna throw up."

I wasn't surprised to hear this because nausea is a common reaction to severe trauma.

I let her talk about it and get out her full story. "How did you handle this crash of your world?" I asked, knowing she would probably say she went to food and maybe alcohol to self-medicate. I also emphasized how cowardly and pathetic it was for Steve to have texted the news to her. Of course she agreed.

Terri looked out the window. She tossed her Kleenex in the trash can and grabbed a new one. "Hmmm…oh, that's right. I slammed the lid on my laptop, got up, and went to the fridge." A pregnant silence echoed through the room, which is part of the therapy process.

"Wow, I've never really seen the connection in a big way. I mean, I always knew I was an emotional eater, but hadn't looked at the cause-effect relationship much," she said.

"So you went to your drug of choice – which is food – for comfort? People do that all the time. We turn to what gives us comfort, even if it's only temporary. Did you binge, or do you even remember, since it was a few years ago?"

"Yeah, I remember making some chocolate chip cookie dough, and gorging myself on the chips at first. Then once I got the dough mixed, I just lost myself in it. It's like I really couldn't stop eating it."

"You were just trying to fix your broken heart with food," I said. "It seems to feel good in the moment, but bingeing can be very violent and angry – almost like a rape of the food. And beneath it all, it was about your heart's longing for love. When someone binges, they shove the food in so fast, they don't really have time to savor its taste. It is filling an empty love tank with food. Although it seems to relieve the pain for a short while, it doesn't fix a broken heart."

"Well, that's kind of a weird way to put it, but it's true. I was looking for love in all the wrong places – I mean, what kind of love can your fridge really give you?"

Terri wrinkled her forehead, "Man, that's so weird. I mean – how can you heal a broken heart with food? It's crazy." She shook her head in disbelief.

"Actually it's pretty common. Every day people self-medicate, trying to fill the holes in their hearts

with food, drugs, alcohol, gambling, shopping –
whatever floats their boats. It's different things for
each person, and often addictions come in pairs."

The heart of every addiction, including food
addiction, is pain in our stories, which we call
trauma. In the case of binge eating disorders, I can
usually go back into the client's story and find out
what happened when they started to gain weight.
This is also a big part of the equation as to why
people relapse. I don't mean that you are ever fully
"recovered," this side of Heaven. It is a continual
struggle and a continual process of attending
meetings and staying in community. Since we were
created for relationship – with God and other people
– there is no substitute.

Addictions – if untreated - end in isolation – the
opposite of relationship. Whether it's anorexia
(which involves a true obsession with food, even
though the person is trying to avoid food,
paradoxically), alcohol, drugs, gambling, computer,
sex addiction, or food addiction, at the tail end the
person no longer cares about much of anything
except her drug of choice. The final stage ends in
profound aloneness, with her drug of choice. She
doesn't care much about relationships because she is
consumed by her drug of choice. But the beauty is

there is always help. Always. Don't let Satan convince you that you'll never get better. That's the grand lie he uses to stop you from trying.

Just what is an addiction? Addiction has three components:

1. Loss of control: The alcoholic, food addict, computer addict, etc. loses control over how much she eats, drinks, or uses the computer. She may want to cut back or quit (if it doesn't involve a food addiction), but can't. Often people cut back to prove to themselves they really are not an alcoholic or addict, but that they could actually quit at any time. But even *trying* to cut back or quit proves that the person knows she has a problem.

2. Tolerance: The amounts of using increase in order to get the same effects. For example, a person with alcohol dependency (on the way to becoming an alcoholic if something is not done) who used to get a buzz off of two glasses of wine is now "needing" three in order to reach the desired effect.

3. High Consequences: Even though there are negative consequences, the

person is unable to stop. For substance addictions, legal issues such as DUIs serve as consequences. Also relationship issues due to the substance. For example, your spouse or parents are concerned and have spoken to you about it. For food addiction, it may be that you have difficulty keeping up with your kids or hiking with your friends. Or you may have acquired diabetes due to weight gain. If you are bulimic, you may have developed problems with your teeth. Or you may have passed out, or you may have had other health issues related to your illness.

Terri continued with her recollection of when she first fell head-over-heels in love with food. She described developing rituals in which she paired particular foods with certain activities. For example, whenever she watched TV, she ate chips. This grew to a point she never watched TV without eating them. Another ritual involved stopping at fast food restaurants to buy milkshakes whenever she drove to the next largest town. Since she drove there about three times a week, she downed three milkshakes a week. Lately, she mentioned, she had started buying fries on her way home from working out. Terri expressed some fear that buying fries could develop into a ritual.

"When your binge from losing Steve was over, do you remember what happened?" I asked her.

"Um, I got back on Facebook and looked at the picture of them again. And that's when I decided I would get skinny because I knew if I was skinny, life would be a breeze. The girl he left me for was probably a size 2 or 4. I knew then that getting skinny was the answer."

She shifted in her chair and crossed her legs. "Oh, and I decided to make myself a margarita." That may have been a hint as to what her second addiction was, and I filed it into the back of my mind. Timing is everything, and I would have to decide whether or not to pursue the avenue of drinking or wait until another day.

Terri only appeared slightly overweight. But I learned long ago that what you see is not really an accurate picture of a woman's size because often women change sizes by either a little or a lot, depending on their life stories.

"So you figured if you could get to a certain weight – a perfect weight – then your whole life would be absolutely perfect?"

She rolled her eyes and laughed nervously. "Man, that's really messed up, isn't it? I mean, it really made sense at the time, and I think probably most of the girls in my high school thought the same way."

"Yeah, it's pretty common for girls and women to feel that way at one time or another. Some women are on a lifelong quest for the perfect diet so they can lose weight and then finally become happy." I thought of many women who had come in over the years who had been in search of the perfect body, which they believed would lead to the perfect life.

"Yeah, that sounds like my mom. She was always on a diet."

Girls absorb their mothers' body image issues like sponges absorb water. Usually if the mother preoccupies herself with body image and food issues, it will have a strong impact on their daughters. The daughters won't necessarily have the same food/body image problems, but the importance of the matter will weigh heavy on their hearts.

I ask, "So what did you do after you vowed to get *skinny*?" The word "skinny" rolls off women's lips like honey. They light up and smile when they talk about getting skinny, as though they will be living in heaven on earth when they reach this nirvana. But this side of heaven, the perfect life cannot be grasped. There is no heaven on earth.

"I decided 100 pounds would be the perfect weight. I figured once I got there, I would get a nice boyfriend, and my life would be great. Things would start to work like a brand new computer with all the latest software." Terri shifted and grabbed the latte she had brought in.

"How did you go about your journey to Skinnyville – or Heaven on earth, as you thought at the time?"

"I had a really strict regimen of what I would eat, and planned it out carefully." She explained the details of a meticulous diet, which I don't care to reveal just in case there are a few readers out there who would decide to copy her regimen. "After about three months, I was a size 0."

Terri was probably about 5 feet 9 inches or so. She definitely qualified as anorexic at the time, whether she admitted it or refused to admit it.

"But then people said I looked sick and I was as flat as a table, so I decided to go up to a size 1."

"Did you have the perfect life?"

Again, Terri laughed nervously because she realized life on earth is not perfect.

"No, I was actually pretty depressed, but I liked

the clothes shopping part. It was fun, although it was kinda hard to find size 1s. But I was really surprised that my phone wasn't ringing a lot because I thought guys would be calling and texting me all the time. And my girlfriends were jealous because they wanted to be skinny."

The floodgates of jealousy open when women lose weight and get closer to our society's distorted view of what beauty is. I only wish other people would see the pain and sadness of their lives rather than covet their size one jeans.

"After that, I decided it wasn't worth it. All this starving and exercising like a maniac to get skinny so I could have the perfect life, and it really didn't pay off. So one night I decided, 'heck with it. I'm gonna make some brownies and pig out on them until I can hardly breathe.' So that's what I did. I started bingeing, which is kinda weird because before I went on my first diet, I never really binged. It seems like it's a vicious cycle that never ends."

"Yeah, you're right," I said. "And the whole thing is really about trying to replace love with food – when you don't feel cared for and loved, you go to food or dieting to try to fill up that huge hole in your heart." She nodded her head in agreement.

As we processed through the big R – the

rejection of this guy that had been very special to her in her broken heart, I asked Terri if she would be willing to make a log of how she was feeling each time she binged. "What do you mean? Usually I'm feeling just kind of yucky when I binge."

"Well, what do you think would happen if you tried to name and write down what you were feeling, and why you felt that when you binged?"

"I don't know. But I'll give it a try. I think I do a lot of eating when I feel bad."

I gave Terri a feelings chart, which included dozens of words under the main categories of mad, sad, glad, fear, lonely and shame. I asked her to put the feelings chart on her refrigerator. It is usually a great reminder for clients to scan their hearts when they graze their kitchens. I figured we would pinpoint some of the trigger feelings that had caused her to eat because she didn't know what else to do with her feelings. Often it is anger, rejection, or sadness. But sometimes it is boredom. Yet every person is individual and has different feelings that trigger binges. And the binge does not have to be food-related. It can be shopping, reading excessively, pornography, computers, TV, gambling, over exercising, or anything else in excess.

That week Terri recorded the feelings she had

when she binged, and when she returned, she said she realized she ate a lot when she felt sad, angry or bored. The next week, I asked her to journal about everything that was bothering her. She could not say 'nothing' because we needed to get to a deeper understanding of what happened to her heart when she was bingeing. So if she truly believed nothing was bothering her, she had to look further to discover what it was.

So often people feel that nothing is bothering them, but they haven't learned the skill of being able to identify their feelings. It can take a lot of work, especially if you grew up in a home where you were not really allowed to have feelings. For example, in a home where if you came home from school crying, your parent(s) would not take the time to comfort you and listen and validate your feelings. Instead they said, "Don't let _____ bother you." The blank could be a person or a situation. The message was your feelings did not matter. Another common phrase is, "You're just oversensitive," in which the child is told not to feel sad or angry or disappointed.

Terri began to talk about some issues she had with her parents. Even though she loved them very much, she believed they treated her harshly as a little girl. We processed these feelings, talking about the fact that even though they love her dearly, they made some mistakes because to be human is to make mistakes. She did so, and reported feeling much better after getting the feelings out.

Of course sometimes people call this psychobabble. But when we read the Psalms, we will note that David often cried out to God about the good, the bad, and the ugly. David would have been diagnosed with many different problems if he were living today. Sometimes we forget that God wants to know our feelings. Of course he already knows them, but he deeply desires to walk and talk with us throughout our days because he longs to connect with us in a personal relationship.

Journaling about our true feelings is a safe way to get them out. Admitting our true emotions is one aspect of the process of being real. Jesus is our model for being authentic or real, because he meant what he said and said what he meant. He did not try to soften what he said, but spoke in a direct way. Since we were created for relationship – with God and with other people – then sharing our feelings or "being real" should be a part of who we are on a daily basis. Even though we don't have the right to brashly spit our feelings all over other people, we do have the responsibility to put forth what is on our hearts.

Terri began to write down each time she turned to food for comfort. She began looking through feeling word lists and became better at simply naming the feelings. At first she would come in and say she had felt yucky, bad, or depressed. She learned she turned to food when she felt angry, rejected or bored. At first she couldn't identify the feelings. But once we teased them apart, she discovered her triggers for over-eating. Like anything else in life, practice makes you better. I know the saying goes, "Practice makes perfect," but by now you know the word "perfect" doesn't set with me very well until we are on the other side of glory.

Gradually we chipped away at the ball of feelings that Terri had never dealt with, as well as things that were going on in her life during the therapy process. Terri got so she could have won an Olympic medal at figuring out what was bothering her, and naming it with one or more feeling words.

Eventually the weight slowly come off. She made a resolution not to go on any more diets, even though it wasn't the New Year. The next week she came in and announced she vowed to continue talking and journaling about what was really bothering her. She planned to do this with God, as well as on paper and with other people that were safe to talk to, and told me her plan was to talk to God first about everything. But at the same time, Terri realized she wouldn't always remember to do that because she was not a perfect human being. She also decided to work more on her relationships with friends. "After all," she said, "life is really about relationships – with God and with people." Her last appointment, she told me she had lost about twenty pounds and she wasn't really concerned about being a certain size anymore. She also had decided that her size 6 goal was not something that she would be able to maintain easily. She had worked through a lot, and I was very proud of her and told her so during her last appointment.

Dahlia, a forty-something client, came in the other day announcing she had joined a particular diet program. We started talking about the four-letter word, diet, and whether or not diets work.

"Sure they do," she said. "I know lots of people who have lost weight." She named various friends and relatives who had lost anywhere from five to fifty pounds on the program.

"How long have they kept the weight off?" I asked.

"Well, it's kind of too early to tell. Most of them just lost the weight over the past six months or so."

"Do you think they will keep it off for the next five, ten, or twenty years?" I asked.

She started to laugh, which in this case was because she felt uncomfortable. "I doubt it." Her gaze dropped to the floor. She twisted a lock of her long auburn hair.

"What if you were to really address the underlying issues of *why* you overeat?" I asked. "We could start with the time of your life when you first put on weight."

"Oh, you mean back in high school? Sure. But really nothing was bothering me back then. Everything was good."

I have heard this so many times. I am not surprised when people deny that nothing of significance was happening when they first began to gain weight.

After talking about this for a while, she realized one thing had changed, and that it had a monumental impact on her. Her older brother had moved away to college that September. She had told me she came from a good Christian family. But as we talked, she casually mentioned her parents argue a lot. In fact, the tension in the family due to all the fighting cast a dark cloud in the air. When her brother was around, they would go downstairs and watch movies or play ping pong when her parents fought, but once he moved to college, she was on her own. As we discussed what this was like, she said she would often stay glued to the TV during the almost daily arguing, and food began to be something she turned to in order to feel better.

This new habit eventually developed into a ritual, and she started to munch on whatever she could find around the house. Sometimes she even stopped at the store on the way home from school to buy the snacks she planned to binge on.

We can easily begin to stalk our fridges in search of comfort or love. In many homes, food is readily available. And if it's not in the house, it is easy to walk or drive to the nearest store. It is no wonder that we have so many overweight people in America.

Once Dahlia realized diets were not long-term solutions, she decided to drop out of the diet program. Now she is committed to working on the issues of her heart that made her turn to food for comfort. For the first time in her life, Dahlia recognizes that issues of her heart lead her to overeat, and she is tackling those issues instead of treating the problem with a diet.

She joined Overeaters Anonymous, which works on heart issues. I wished Dahlia a lovely journey as she remodeled her heart and began working – for the first time in her life – the root causes of her battle with overeating. I expect to hear from her again when she loses the weight. Because this time, it probably won't find her again.

Chapter 9

Oh, to be a Kitty!

Great news! Chocolate has superb anti-aging properties. At least that's what I read while waiting for my kitty's appointment at the vet. If I keep drinking mochas at the same rate, I should reclaim my 29th birthday by Memorial Day! I guess I will keep feeding the chocolate monster within. Maybe I should get back into the habit of making chocolate chip cookie dough. I used to mix it up every few weeks, but hardly any of it made it into the oven because it would take a detour and end up in my tummy.

While I thought about this delectable news about chocolate, the vet assistant called us in. Prissy, my kitty, needed booster shots. It's still hard to believe I have a cat because I thought of myself as a dog-only type of person. But my husband wanted a kitty, so what could I say? She is loving - most of the time, low-maintenance, and makes an excellent heating pad.

The vet assistant weighed Prissy before checking her vitals. Then she brought her back into the exam room. A few minutes later, the vet entered.

The last time we saw the vet, he scolded me because Prissy plumped up to eighteen pounds. He said at that weight, she could develop serious health conditions. So he suggested I reduce her food. I cut her back gradually, a little each week. Let me tell you, Prissy became nasty when she felt deprived. She spent her time hanging out by the pantry door where the cat food is kept, making noises like she was in labor. Today the good news was she has lost a little over two pounds. The vet now wants her to lose about two more pounds, then she will be at her so-called ideal weight.

The advantage Prissy has over you and me is she has no psychological hang-ups about the number on the scale. She doesn't compare herself with other kitties, thinking, *is that cat's butt bigger or smaller than mine?* Or, *When I take a selfie, do I look okay?* She has no concerns about her appearance because she is preoccupied with more important things like pouncing on our dog or looking for bugs on the ceiling. I have seen no evidence she obsesses about her waist or the appearance of any other body parts.

She doesn't care about her size or shape, but is more concerned about keeping herself clean. Oh, to be a kitty!

What kind of freedom would you have if you lived more like Prissy? I don't mean having claws and a mousie toy, but what if you could be totally without knowledge or concern about your appearance? Maybe that gives you shudders, and you picture yourself as a sloth rolling out of bed with bad breath, putting on a little pit juice (deodorant), and going about your day. Your hair is uncombed and your clothes wrinkled, but you don't care. You're on a mission to live life with gusto. For Prissy, that means hunting down breakfast. But for you, it means developing your gifts and talents to bless others.

Most teen girls and women frequently compare their bodies with other people. Some – not all, but some – of these girls and women you compare yourself with have eating disorders you can't see. Other times women and girls compare themselves with magazines pictures, which leads to toxic thoughts. They feel they don't measure up. We have already discussed the statistics on this, which reveals females feel more body shame when they peruse magazines.

I normally avoid looking at such magazines. I

don't need that kind of negative influence in my thinking. I am reminded of the passage in Philippians 4:8. Although it wasn't written with body image issues in mind, Paul attests: "Finally, brothers, whatever is true, whatever is noble, whatever is right, whatever is pure, whatever is lovely, whatever is admirable, think about such things."

It is not healthy to stuff our feelings, as I often tell my clients. In fact I tell them stuffing is for turkeys and teddy bears, and they are neither one! Neither are you. So it is important to communicate your feelings in a safe venue, perhaps with a trusted friend who is not shaming or even on paper because paper doesn't judge. (If you are concerned about someone finding it, no worries because you can type it and then delete it.) Believe it or not, the act of the purging your feelings is the important thing. King David called out to God again and again, and often expressed his deepest feelings.

Focusing on other peoples' bodies and shaming ourselves for our own looks is not true, noble, right, pure, lovely, or admirable. But rather the pictures often lead us to feeling down. They bring us down and is another form of "stinking thinking'" as 12-step recovery programs say.

Notice Scripture does *not* say, "Look at the

woman (or teenager) in front of you in line at Wal-Mart. Notice if her thighs, waist, bust, ankles, and/or derriere is bigger or smaller than yours. Then mope around for the next four months because you feel fat and ugly compared to her." Thank goodness it doesn't say that! We are not supposed to compare ourselves to the world's standards, because we are actually citizens of heaven. That's why Scripture emphasizes, "Man looks at outward appearance, but God looks at the heart" (1 Samuel 16:7b). How I wish we could saturate the hearts and minds of girls and women with this profound truth. You probably noticed the verse says nothing about evaluating ourselves on the basis of our body fat percentage, or on the shapeliness of our figures. What a sigh of relief.

Since the Bible focuses little on our physical appearance, does this mean we have permission to let our bodies go? To eat whatever we want, or to starve ourselves to an unhealthy size until our monthly periods trickle down and stop? Of course not.

Scripture *does* speak about our bodies. We are called to take loving care of them because they are temples of God. Our bodies are temples of the Holy Spirit. First Corinthians 3:16 says, "Do you not know that your body is a temple of the Holy Spirit, and that God's Spirit lives in you?"

How can we honor God with our bodies? For me, this means treating them with respect. This is where good nutrition, exercise, sleep, and general care for our bodies come into the picture. If we treat our bodies like landfills, filling them with whatever we feel like on a regular basis, we are doing so to the temple of God.

We fall into a habit of sizing up the shapes of other women and girls to see if we're skinnier, fatter, flabbier, or shapelier. Sometimes we even try to guess what size of clothes they wear and/or their weight. Once we begin to develop body awareness, we start to think and ruminate on what we look like.

In past decades, women became conscious of their bodies at an older age. What precise age that was depended on the person and the culture, and still does to some extent. But today many young girls around the age of four and five are making comments about their bodies about feeling fat and wanting to be sexy. That is terribly sad and frightening at the same time.

Women tend to think about their bodies about 100 times per day. We glance at ourselves and sometimes even study ourselves whenever we come across reflective surfaces. That includes mirrors, windows, and even toasters. Of course some of us are more obsessed with this than others.

I am thankful my parents often told me if I compared myself with other people, I would always find some who were better in a specific category, as well as others who were worse in that category. This applied to grades, swimming, playing the flute, and just about everything else. When I swam my first swimming race and beat one of the fastest girls in the county, I was prepared that at some point I would lose. This helped me to develop other skills and strengths. Because of this, I have a wide variety of interests. Another gift from that mentality was that I pursued my passions and did not simply do whatever came naturally because of being good at it.

This is probably why I'm more concerned with using my God-given gifts and talents than becoming the best in any category. Even so, I would like to be more like my kitty as far as being oblivious to thinking about my body. Granted, Prissy is much happier now that she can get back up on her cat tree like a gymnast in the Kitty Olympics, if there was such a thing. For a while she couldn't climb up due to her weight.

But women and girls are so brainwashed by our looks-obsessed culture that we continue to evaluate our bodies as a whole as well as in part. We often forget about the internal and focus on the external. Yet it is interesting to note that in the New Testament, external beauty is not mentioned except in the context of playing it down. Instead, personality characteristics are emphasized. The New Testament shifts our attention to our hearts and the internal rather than the external. And true beauty is defined by becoming more Christ-like – exhibiting more of the fruit of the Spirit: love, joy, peace, patience, kindness, faithfulness, gentleness, and self-control (Galatians 5:22).

Whenever we fight the battle of lookism, we recover a bit of what the Body Image Bandit has stolen. The one who would like to kill, steal, and destroy our feelings about ourselves loses ground as we take steps to grasp onto our internal beauty.

I wonder what would happen if we prayed for revival each time we caught ourselves obsessing about other peoples' appearances. Mountains would be moved if hundreds and possibly thousands of people did this. But instead of using our valuable time to focus on prayer and revival, we are self-absorbed. Picture what would happen if we replaced absolutely every thought about calories, fat, our bodies, and how we look with a prayer. Heaven would flood with prayers! I get pumped just thinking about it!

Take the challenge today, and email this to your friends as well. Since women think of their bodies over a hundred times per day, this would be powerful. All the energy we use thinking about calories, our bellies, and what diet to go on next would be drowned out by prayer.

A few years ago while studying the Old Testament, I closely examined the Ten Commandments. The tenth commandment, in particular, caught my attention: "You shall not covet anything that belongs to your neighbor." This intrigued me because I didn't think I was a materialistic sort of person. Then I realized I do obsess about my body at times, and sometimes wish I looked like someone else.

So I began to chew on this whole idea of covetousness and realized I may not covet my neighbor's house or ox – I don't think I've ever seen an ox. None of my neighbors have them, and I doubt yours do either. But my coveting problem is more about bodies than material objects. And I bet if you were to be nakedly honest, you would admit you struggle with this as well.

"Neither shall you covet your neighbor's wife. Neither shall you desire your neighbor's house, or field, or male or female slave, or ox, or donkey, or anything that belongs to your neighbor," Deuteronomy 5:21. (Also see Exodus 20:17.) I certainly don't covet any of my neighbors' spouses. Every once in a while I do see a house I would like, but the last phrase about "anything that belongs to your neighbor" is a biggie. The Hebrew translations do not mention anything about the size of your neighbor's hips or lips. But I think the general idea of longing for anything your neighbor has can certainly lead to a heavy heart, toxic thoughts, discouragement, and disappointment.

What does the word 'covet' actually mean? According to my online dictionary, the first definition of the word is to "want somebody else's property," or more specifically, "to have a strong desire to possess something that belongs to somebody else. The second definition says, "yearn to have," as in "to want to have something very much."

If we look at the word 'covet' in either of those terms, most American women have coveted and continue to covet the bodies of models or people who look like models. Some may do so only periodically, but others do so many times per day. Each time you are in line at the store and out of habit compare the people in front of you to yourself you slip into the realm of coveting. Whenever you find yourself guessing or wondering someone's size or weight, you enter the realm of coveting. You may be in church and notice someone in front of you and notice yourself contemplating what size she wears, you have slithered into the realm of coveting. Or you may wonder what you look like from the back, as other people behind you are seeing you. I know this is the stinking thinking we can easily slip into because I've certainly done so myself.

Backing up to the second commandment, we land on a topic that isn't discussed much nowadays. That is, the dangerous jungle of idolatry. After the prelude of "You shall have no other gods before me," we read the second one, concerning idolatry. "You shall not make for yourself an idol in the form of anything in heaven above or on the earth beneath or in the waters below," states the second commandment. Today, we normally don't have carved images inside our homes which we bow to on a regular basis. (Although many people are worshippers of stuff and are chasing the American Dream like a starving PMS-ing woman chases donuts. I am writing another book about this called, *Stalking the American Dream: The Price Tag of Success*. But that is an entirely different subject.)

More likely, we are bound to have idols in our

minds. These are idols that glisten the covers of magazines and dazzle the screens of our TVs and computers. They also frolic in the forefront of our minds and occupy way too much space of our internal hard drives. Maybe it is time for us to re-think the concept of idolatry and fast forward into the twenty-first century. We have let the winds of our culture sink into our hearts and paint the way we think of our bodies with glasses that are smudged with the grimy crud that make us feel like we don't measure up to the air-brushed, photo shopped images of people who are not real. They are facades. Perfect, flawless, and fake.

Once we begin to obsess about our bodies and focus on refining them into beautiful masterpieces, we have definitely crossed the line and entered into the ungodly land of Idolatry. We are concentrating on carving out the absolute perfect packaging from our natural physiques. This is clearly not about love or giving glory to God. It is about self, and the desire to be worshipped, on some level. It flows out of the longing for others to turn their heads toward us, and for them to say, "Wow. What a beautiful woman." This is a form of worship, and therefore qualifies as idolatry.

I once was obsessed with my body to the point of

spending hours and hours each week sculpting it into a work of art. But as I explained earlier, it backfired on me because the attention I received overwhelmed me.

When do we cross the line from attempting to get healthier to idolatry? Is that when you take one more spin (exercise bike) class per week than you really need? Probably. Could it be when you jog up a steep trail not for health, but to sculpt your legs into ones that will turn heads? Probably. Is it when you starve yourself so that you can get down to a size so you can be the "skinniest" woman in your group of friends? Probably. Or is it when you lose weight because you know that your body fat percentage puts you more at risk for a stroke? Probably not. Is it when you try to lower your body fat percentage so that your arthritis doesn't carry extra weight? I doubt it – unless you already have a low body fat percentage.

The Israelites grew impatient while they waited for Moses to return from the mountain. So they complained to Aaron, Moses' brother. Aaron felt pressured and asked the men to bring him gold jewelry from the women and children. Then he placed the gold into the fire, and later said, "Out came a calf." It is funny when you think about his comment. The idea that, poof, all the sudden a calf emerged – as if he played no part in the situation. This was idolatry because the people put their faith in Aaron and in the golden calf idol instead of trusting in God.

Nowadays we don't enter into this type of worship. (Our society does worship material objects, however.) Yet we worship the human body in many ways. We do it culturally as well as individually. Those in our society who have fit bodies are placed on a pedestal. Is that a form of worship? Certainly.

One of my clients lost twenty-five pounds and received a great deal of praise from her friends and family. Yet several months prior when she earned a large promotion, few of those same people raved about it.

Beauty and fitness receive a grand proportion of kudos from others, while intelligence – especially among women – receives little praise. Appearance and exercise have become idols of sorts in our culture. We worship the physique of those who have excellent bodies according to our culture. Americans are as guilty of idolatry in this sense as the people in the Old Testament.

Hopefully I can become more like my kitty, Prissy, from whom I have learned great things: don't covet other peoples' bodies, and be comfortable in your own skin. Relax, kick back, play, and especially – don't worry about what you look like. Oh, to be a kitty!

Chapter 10

The Man on the Moon – No, I Mean the Chicken Diet

I wasn't sure I heard him right. A physician came into counseling for help with anxiety and depression. He told me during one of our first sessions he was going on a chicken diet.

"A *chicken* diet?" I asked.

"Yeah, I think chicken is the perfect food in lots of ways. If I eat mostly chicken and drink water, then I can lose some of this." He grabbed a glob of excess fat around his belly. Although he could afford to lose a few pounds, Ben was not obese. He looked as though he had once been athletic, and wore a crisp blue shirt that brought attention to his blue eyes. Crossing his legs, Ben placed a few stray strands of dark hair behind his ear.

Still somewhat confused, I said, "That sounds

interesting." I had taken a number of nutrition classes in college, and this chicken and water diet did not sound balanced, especially for a physician. Maybe there was more to his plan.

"No, I've done the research, and I know I can meet my goal in two months at the normal recommended two pounds a week pace. I'll have chicken for breakfast, lunch, dinner, and I'll drop the weight like a woman with PMS drops her boyfriends." We both laughed.

"So you'll have chicken shakes for breakfast, baked chicken nuggets for lunch, and a slab of chicken breast for dinner?" I smiled, thankful it wasn't me that would be eating chicken until I started to look like one. I like chicken, a lot, but can't imagine eating only chicken for a day, let alone three months. Chocolate – sure. But *chicken*? Never.

Ben nervously picked up and set down his empty Starbucks cup. Was he anxious about his first counseling appointment or his outlandish diet, knowing I was about to ask him more questions?

"It's gonna be great," he said, "I'll drop my extra weight, and then I can wear cool clothes. The women will be really into me." He smiled and looked out the window as though he had found the answer to all of life's problems. The Great Fix. The Magical Cure.

"So then you'll have the perfect life?" I asked, without any shame in my tone of voice. Countless women told me that when they got skinny, they would buy cute clothes. I usually asked them why they wouldn't buy the clothes until they were skinny, but they scrunched up their noses and thought it was absurd. In fact, many people use the word 'skinny' as a magical word. They get so excited about the little pet word, their mouths automatically form into broad smiles when saying it. Once they are *skinny*, their lives will suddenly become supremely enjoyable, but not one minute before. They realize cute clothes are available in larger sizes now, but they have no interest in spending money on them until they are – *skinny.*

The magical thinking creates a life of its own. Life begins after they lose weight. Then guys will want to date them, which will lead to a boyfriend. Not just any boyfriend, but a perfect- or almost perfect boyfriend, which would open the golden door to the Perfect Life. Once the door opens, they will create a lovely wedding, and later a beautiful home. Finally they have children, and as long as they stay skinny, their lives will be flawless, dreamy, and perfect. Because of course their marriages and children will be perfect! Or so they believe.

Magical thinking comes in many different flavors: Once I earn a college degree, life will be perfect. Or once I marry, life will be perfect. Or once I have a house or a larger house, life will be perfect. Or another popular version: Once I move to _____, life will be perfect.

So once again I found myself talking to a man with a mission to change his whole world – this time through the chicken diet. "Will you eat anything besides chicken, or just chicken?" I asked.

He bent his elbows, locked his hands, and placed them in back of his head, which often happens when men (and sometimes women) feel out of control. "Well, I'll eat mostly chicken, and take a supplement liquid diet to get some more nutrients, with maybe a salad or piece of fruit once in a while." His leg began to bounce up and down, which told me he felt anxious. Ben felt uncomfortable talking about this because he started to wonder if the chicken diet really would make his life a trip to Disneyland.

Now both of his legs bounced lightly. "I need to lose weight fast so I can lose it all before summer. Then I can get a gorgeous girlfriend and we can enjoy ourselves water skiing and hiking. I mean she has to be smart too and funny and all, but anyway then I can have an awesome summer."

"Do you think people usually keep weight off when they lose it quickly on diets?"

He laughed, but it was a nervous laugh and not a funny laugh. "Usually diets don't work anyway. But research shows that the slower you lose weight, the longer you usually keep it off." We both laughed because we realized he was about to contradict his own beliefs by going on a diet. And not just any diet – a *chicken* diet.

"So are you telling me you don't really believe in what you are about to do?"

He started to rub the part of the couch where his hand had been resting, which is another sign of anxiety.

"Yeah, I guess so." He looked at the floor and then out the window.

"When did you first start to gain weight?" I asked the million-dollar question that most health professionals never ask.

"Hmmm … I think it was my second year of med school. Before that I was pretty buff and worked out a lot. I kept working out, but started packing on the pounds."

"So what happened in your life the second year of med school?"

"Oh, nothing really. I mean it was brutal and

agonizing, but nothing really happened that year. I did well in all my classes, and had some good friends I hung out with."

"So nothing else significant happened during that time of your life?" I wondered if maybe the stress had caused him to turn to food as his drug of choice. But I wasn't about to give up. My work is similar to being a detective. Sometimes I have to dig for clues. I had a gut feeling something of significance had happened during that time, and Ben had no idea how much weight the event carried in his heart.

"Nope. Everything stayed the same. I mean, my girlfriend dumped me for someone else, but we hadn't really been together that long." People often drop bombs like this in therapy, not realizing the tremendous impact the bomb made on their lives.

I sensed he had cared deeply for her, even though the relationship had not lasted long. "What was her name?" I asked.

"Brenda," he said, in a quiet voice which spoke volumes.

"What was she like?" People often think if they talk about painful situations, they will feel worse. But usually the opposite is true. Yet it is a tightrope because if they get overwhelmed, they may get flooded sort of like a car. Then they can't function.

But if they continue to stuff their feelings, it's like trying to hold a beach ball underwater. It's only a matter of time before the pressure causes the ball to pop out of the water with a burst of power. If we stuff our feelings, we often self-medicate with excessive food, drugs, computer time, shopping, working out, alcohol, sex addiction or even reading excessively as a form of escape.

"She was really smart – another med student, actually. And so pretty, but not in a model sort of way. More of the natural, girl-next-door type. She had this auburn hair that was curly, and she hated it. But it's one of the things that made her special. And she had a laugh that you could hear from here to Singapore." He smiled quickly, then it vanished like a light switch that flicked on for a millisecond.

"She sounds like an amazing woman," I said.

He sighed, which I learned years ago usually means something important is about to be said. "Then she became lab partners with my roommate – the lab partners were assigned to us – and they gradually went from lab partners to life partners." He looked at the floor as though his eyes could bore a hole to the depths of the earth.

"I am *so* sorry," I said. I could feel the tears welling up in my own heart and saw one of his flowing down his cheek. We continued to talk gently about Brenda, and I acknowledged it was very hard to do, but told him that he couldn't get through the pain unless he was willing to work through the trauma to gain freedom from its power.

I realized Ben was getting overwhelmed and wanted to lighten the moment so he wouldn't get flooded and decide not to come back. "Hey, I have a question," I said.

"Oh brother – you *always* have a question, don't you?" We both laughed.

"What's that?" he asked.

"Well, you said you were in great shape at that time of your life. But even so, it didn't get you the perfect life. What's that about?"

He laughed, this time a funny laugh. "Sheesh – you always nail me, don't you? Okay, okay, I'll admit that even though I was in great shape, it wasn't the magic cure-all." We talked about some things in his life he was looking forward to because I wanted him to feel grounded before leaving. If people leave when they are flooded with sadness, they can spiral downward, which can lead to more depression and/or self-medication.

I suspected Ben probably struggled with an addiction to pornography. The reason I thought so was because he had some similarities with men who often have this problem and/or other types of sex addiction. He had a people-pleasing type of personality, meaning he tried to make people happy as much as possible. I could already sense he went to great lengths to avoid conflict. This stemmed from some abandonment issues, probably in his childhood. I figured that one or both parents were unavailable in some way - either emotionally or physically. This could be due to death, divorce, workaholism, alcoholism, or another reason.

Another characteristic he had which is often a characteristic of pornography/sex addicts (in men) is that he is an over-achiever. This is not necessarily true for women, although women certainly can have pornography/sex addiction as well.

The third quality that made me suspect a pornography problem was Ben had experienced a profound rejection by the opposite sex. Even though he said they were not together long, Brenda's rejecting him scarred his heart, which men often try to fill with pornography to the point it develops into an addiction. After all, a real relationship requires work and sacrifice, but a "relationship" with a piece of paper or an image on a phone or computer screen takes no work. No honey-do lists, no talking through difficulties, and no conflict. Because pornography is readily and anonymously obtained via the internet, it is often used to soothe pain.

The fourth quality I wasn't sure about was whether or not Ben had issues with his father. Often men who are addicted to pornography have relationships with their fathers that are shallow. Their fathers - for one reason or another - did not give them the blessing of saying, "I'm so proud of you, son." This burns a crater in the heart of a man, and in a twisted way, he tries to fill up that hole with women. The women may be real or virtual. That is the heart of a pornography or sex addict. Since they are not involved with a real person in this respect, they think they are immune from rejection. After all, a person who doesn't really exist or is not really in your life can't abandon or reject you. No wonder experts call internet pornography "the crack cocaine of sex addiction."

Eventually Ben admitted he started using pornography on a regular basis at about the same time Brenda left him, although he had begun using it when he was thirteen and his dad left his mom for another woman. Just as I suspected, Ben had an addiction to pornography. He used it for stress relief, he used it because he felt like he worked hard and deserved it (entitlement), and he used it because it had become a ritual. And other times he used it because he was bored.

Strikingly, Ben used pornography for many of the same reasons many people use food: it is easier to turn to an image than to risk sharing your feelings with another, it's a form of entitlement, and as a way to de-stress.

An interesting fact about pornography addiction and eating disorders is that they are two sides of a coin. Women get entrapped into a mindset that if they have the perfect body, life will be perfect. And men perpetuate that belief by getting entranced into a mindset that the perfect woman has a thin body with relatively large breasts.

Eating disorders and pornography addiction feed each other. Women feel great pressure to be thin and sexy because our culture floods them with a tsunami of images which stress that beauty is almost everything. And of course thinness is valued as a major component of beauty. Men (as well as some women) pore over the images for the purposes of self-medication. And so pornography addiction and eating disorders – especially bulimia and anorexia – are two beasts entangled in a venomous cycle like a dog chasing its tail.

I enjoyed working with Ben, but realized he would benefit more from therapy with a CSAT, which stands for Certified Sex Addiction Therapist. Thankfully, Ben agreed to see the CSAT therapist.

At the last appointment, Ben handed me a brown paper bag. "Hey, I brought you something," he said with a grin. I opened it, and inside was a rubber chicken, about six inches long. "That's to show your clients that if they have magical thinking – with diets or anything else – it's like putting their faith in a rubber chicken." I laughed and wished him success on his journey.

Chapter 11

Mama Mia!

How Mothers Influence Body Image

When I lived on Maui, I bodysurfed several times a week. One day the surf at Makena Beach was exceptionally high – the highest I ever remembered. I heard a man further out in the surf shout as loud as a lion, "MAMA MIA!" I turned my neck to see the tallest wave I had ever seen. And it was about ready to swallow us up. Forever.

The next thing I remember, I tumbled up and down and all around, spinning and trying to figure out which way was up. I couldn't get my bearings because I felt like I was in a washing machine. The ultimate goal was survival as I felt the power of the magnificent Pacific Ocean push and pull my body in a thousand different directions.

Some way, thank the Lord, I survived.

Maybe you're feeling like the cultural wave of negative body image messages are thoroughly overwhelming, like this mama mia sized wave. But there is always hope. Together, we can beat that bad dude I call the Body Image Bandit.

I asked my Facebook friends to share their stories about how their mothers impacted their own body image, and received numerous responses. One of them came from a woman in her sixties whom I'll call Sally. Sally's mother feared getting fat more than almost anything else. She projected the fear onto Sally, and made Sally take diet pills in junior high. Once she grew up and married, Sally continued to navigate the line between enjoying eating with her husband and controlling her weight. Women gain an average of 18 pounds during the first year of marriage. They grow discouraged to move from their pre-wedding weight to their rounder, settled-in weight.

During her second pregnancy, Sally experienced morning sickness, which resulted in weight loss. Eventually she developed bulimia. During her studies at nursing school, she realized bulimia was destroying her from within and decided to seek treatment.

Bulimia is a wolf in sheep's clothing, as I seems

harmless on the surface, but causes organ damage, severe tooth decay and other health problems.

Even at age 95, Sally's mother continued to obsess about her own weight and appearance, even though she had been quite ill for several years.

The trenches of our body image issues run deep, not even lessening in our old age or during a lengthy illness. Even with dementia, many women's love/hate relationships with their bodies and food cause great distress as they continue to obsess about how they look. The desire to be thin is a constant dose of poison our culture feeds us day in and day out to the point we lose touch with our normal, natural, womanly bodies.

Another friend in her fifties emailed me about her mother's toxic influence on her body image. This friend, whom I will call Katie, is an attractive woman who gained sixty pounds since college. She modeled for Macys and Saks Fifth Avenue while in her twenties. One day around that time, a stranger said to Katie, "You are *so* beautiful!" Katie's mom overheard, and commented, "You are *not* beautiful! You are *fat!*" But here is the clincher: Katie was a size 0 at the time.

A few months later, Katie's grandparents visited and her grandfather said, "Katie, you are quite the beauty, and I am so proud of you!" Since Katie graduated from nursing school, her grandfather was referring to Katie's intelligence and her physical beauty. Katie's mom overheard this conversation, and she flew into a rage, saying her grandfather's words had no meaning.

When Katie's mother pointed out her flaws, they froze into Katie's memory. From that day forward she scrutinized her body for flaws and imperfections.

Katie continues her story, "Now I am fat, for real, and I know it to the bones. But along this route I came to see that I am much more than what I look like."

I received another email from a friend I'll call Marisol. Marisol, in her forties, says, "First I will say, I know I am in charge of myself now … but wow, did my mom influence me, and I am very heavy and kind of secretly blame her … even though I am a grown up.

"My mom was always 10 to 20 pounds overweight after having three kids, and she was beautiful - sort of like Doris Day. She dieted, exercised, and complained daily about her appearance, saying her clothes were too tight, and craved compliments about her looks. If she received a comment that she was pretty, she would be happy for the whole day." Like many other women, she let the scale or a compliment dictate whether she would have a good day or a bad day.

"Mom put me on a diet at age 12, and from 12 until I turned 30, when I had to tell her to leave me alone, my weight was her issue. Putting me on a diet was the worst thing she could have done to my regular kid-sized body. She took her own issues with food and body image out on me, and projected them onto me. I remember my stepdad and mom arguing about it. He thought it was stupid the way she was so obsessed about my body."

Mothers frequently perceive their daughters' bodies as extensions of their own. They project their own food and body struggles onto their daughters and attempt to control their daughters' bodies. Their own fear of fat becomes the focal point of their daughter's body image, which prevents their daughters from developing healthy relationships with food and with their daughter's own bodies. Their mothers' imprint gets branded into their heads.

Thinking about this subject inspired me to write a blog entry called, "It Loves Me, It Loves Me Not: Your Relationship with Your Scale." It was posted on my blog, which is called, "Tooshiebog.com." I decided to include it here because women have love/hate relationships with their scales, and often let those relationships dictate whether they have good days or bad days. So here it is:

It Loves Me, It loves Me Not

What would happen if we stopped our all-or-nothing, black and white thinking? What if we re-trained ourselves to look at life more as it truly is – in terms of grays more than black or white? As far as body image is concerned, this would mean that we stop weighing ourselves. Some people are so obsessed with the scale, its numbers haunt them throughout their lives. Do you give your scale the power to own your soul? Over the past several years counseling women, I have encountered many who give their scales that much power. Other women have sadly expressed their mothers did this, which profoundly impacted their growing up years. If their mothers weighed in at a lower number, they displayed a fun, upbeat side. But if the cloud of weight gain (even a pound or two) hung in the air, the house felt tense and their moms behaved depressed and moody.

Eating disorder programs usually recommend that their patients get rid of their scales. They realize many of their clients have an obsession with weighing themselves, often stepping on their scales many times per day. Experts believe people can tell whether they are gaining or losing weight by the way their clothes fit. Besides, weight varies throughout the day, week, and month (according to the menstrual cycle) normally anyway.

How long will you continue to let your scale cause you to have bad days, weeks, and months? Can you honestly say you never let the number on the scale – the magic number- influence how you treat people?

Try This: Write a letter to your scale. Explain how you have given it too much power in your life (i.e.

letting it dictate on many days whether you have a good day or a bad day). Describe its influence in your life. You may even want to give it a name, and suggest that it go on vacation. Or better yet – move out.

Among the messages I received from Facebook friends, I read a surprising one from a friend I attended high school with. Celine had always been slender, and she stated her mom had often called her "pleasantly plump." This surprised me because she always looked slender.

Celine's mother also said she was "big boned," and said she would never have a flat stomach.

As I write this, I remember an exercise used at some eating disorder clinics. Each client receives a large ball of string. She is asked to cut a length of string she thinks accurately shows her waist measurement, without actually measuring. After cutting the string, she sets it aside. Next, she is asked to cut a length of string around her waist by using the string itself to "measure." When she compares the two strings, usually she finds a significant difference between the real and the perceived. She believes she is much larger than the string measures.

I imagine Celine's mom saw her own body as much larger than it actually was. Then she projected this inaccurate perception onto her daughter.

Celine vowed to "never ever utter the words, 'pleasantly plump' or 'big-boned' to my kids. And I never have." Fat shaming, as that type of language is now called, doesn't work anyway. It usually has the opposite effect. In other words, people give up and eat even more.

Another friend wrote she had no problems with body image until she started developing. Her mom told her she ate too many cookies, which made her hips broaden. The focus shifted from her personality, gifts, and talents to her appearance. Her value was defined by her looks from that point forward. Celine began to constantly compare her body with those of other women.

When I think of Celine's story, I think of how clients relive their own issues when their daughters reach the age of their own abuse (or the divorce of their parents or another major trauma in their lives). Sometimes this results in over-protectiveness in which the daughter is rarely allowed to leave the house. Other times this means the mothers assume every man could inflict abuse upon their daughters, which promotes major mistrust of men.

Another friend sent me an email that said her stepdad called her, "The child that ruined my wife's body." As I read those words, I imagined the punch in the gut those words must have been.

Another friend, whom I'll call Karen, remembers her brother calling her "fat." After that, Karen vowed to do whatever it took to get into a pair of size 6 Calvin Klein jeans. Most women who struggle with eating disorders remember this type of significant moment in their stories. Her vow included starving herself to the point she passed out on a beach. When she regained consciousness, the paramedic asked her, "What can I do to prevent this from happening to my daughter?" With tears in her eyes, she answered, "You can love her unconditionally."

What exactly did Karen mean by that? Often this means her heart cries out because of growing up in a shame-based family. In other words, she may have come from a family with minimal praise but many "shoulds." The "should" list greatly outweighed the praise list, and the message received by her heart is she does not deserve love because she is not good enough. "Don't do this, don't do that," is the general feeling in the house. In many ways, she feels little or no freedom to be a child. The freedom to play, explore, and relax is choked by an unending list of "shoulds." The message is the child or teen should try to be as perfect as possible, and the better she or he can be, the more love she receives.

Unfortunately, she believes if she doesn't meet the mark, she is unlovable and flawed. So off she gallops into the wind where she will chase after her dream – her dream of achieving skinnihood. Because deep down she believes thinness is the ticket to love. The perfectionism has slipped into the heart where she will try to be thin forever to obtain the love she craves. All the shoulds have grown great weeds inside of her to create a dark despair that threatens to eat her up. Her parents view their actions as helpful. Yet the unattainable reach for perfectionism has pushed Karen into the arms of an eating disorder.

People think of perfectionism as an asset, and in some ways it is. I am a recovering perfectionist. But have you ever known someone completely engulfed by perfectionism to the point they live in a prison where they can never be good enough? If we are drowning in shame because we feel we don't measure up and we are not good enough, we are stifled. Thankfully, God loves us just as we are. He has the capacity to love us unconditionally, which is hard to grasp. He has paid for everything we have ever done that didn't measure up, as well as all the things we should have done but didn't. He knew we would never measure up when he created us, and he loves us anyway. God loves us so deeply, we can't grasp its vastness. If you can, listen to the song, "How He Loves," by the David Crowder Band. Make sure you listen to the whole song to feel how he describes the profound beauty and power of God's love.

Regardless of your actions, God truly loves you through and through just as you are right now in this moment! He will not love you more if you lose your love handles or your muffin top, or if your skin looks flawless. In fact he knows your heart is flawed and that you have a sin nature, and for that reason he has paved a way to a relationship with him through the cross. Really, you don't have to do anything else because you cannot get into heaven by being good. Ephesians 2:8–9 says, "For it is by grace you have been saved through faith-and this is not from yourselves, it is the gift of God-not by works, so that no one can boast." All you need to do is ask.

Jesus has taken care of the fact that we can never be perfect until we are on the other side of glory. So while we fix our eyes on him, we take the spotlight off ourselves and onto what God essentially cares about. "And let us run with perseverance the race marked out for us, fixing our eyes on Jesus, the perfector of faith." Our culture feeds us horrific lies.

But that is not the heart of God. Like we already discussed, "Man looks at outward appearance, but God looks at the heart." What if we were to take all the energy and time spent obsessing about our bodies and pour it into what God really cares about? After all, Scripture says in Psalm 37:4 "Delight yourselves in the Lord and he will give you the desires of your heart."

This psalm invites us to shift the focal point from self to the cross. We can trade in the pursuit of the perfect body in exchange for fulfilling our maker's purpose for our lives. And with that, we are called to ride the tailwind of God. We use our time visiting the sick, reaching out to others who are hurting rather than spending inordinate amounts of time chasing after the perfect body. After all, the perfect body was only a means to an end. Deep down, you really believed the perfect body was a first class seat to the perfect life, which would be filled with people who loved you. But that was a lie.

We live in a decaying world, and this world suffers a great deal of damage as a result. Pain, sickness, sin, broken relationships, addictions, eating disorders, terrorism, and other tragedies create pain.

The fulfillment and joy we thought would come from attaining an amazing body does not come from a perfect body at all. It comes from walking hand in hand with Jesus every day, grasping onto his glorious grace. But even then, he promised we would have troubles.

Once again, when we go back to Karen's story and what her heart longed for, we can see that eating disorders are relationship issues. In other words, we are all created for relationship – with God and with people. When we don't receive the unconditional love we need, our so-called "love tank" is empty. We feel unlovable, unworthy, and inadequate in one way or another. This often leads to depression, self-medicating, cutting, and/or eating disorders.

"I can't believe these elephant thighs," you remark in front of the mirror as you try on a new pair of jeans. Your daughter hears you, and you both laugh. But these types of negative body image statements thread their poisonous barbs through her entire life story. Such comments- even if said in jest- reinforce the belief in our culture which screams, "If your body isn't perfect, you are shameful."

This spurs girls, sometimes starting before age five, into dieting. Then they begin the cycle of dieting and later bingeing because they feel starved. This leads to shame, which circles back to dieting. Even if they shrink to a normal size, they feel fat. If they have people-pleasing, perfectionist personalities, they often get swallowed up with anorexia. If they are not people-pleasers, they often flirt with throwing up until it develops into full-blown bulimia. But when they purge, they are actually attempting to purge all the hurtful feelings stored in their hearts. This is why learning to express true feelings is so important.

Here are some ways you can try to protect your daughter (or son, as more and more boys are developing eating disorders) from eating disorders:

- Avoid talking about dieting, fat, or your body parts. Whenever you do this, your daughter hears the message that her value rests on how thin she is.
- Discourage dieting, as it usually leads to a lifelong obsession with black-and-white thinking in regards to food.
- Discourage your daughter from looking at beauty and fashion magazines.
- Stop praising girls for their beauty. Instead, focus on their other strengths and accomplishments, When we praise girls for

their appearance, we reinforce the cultural tsunami of lies that drown girls in feelings their value is based on appearance.

- Be aware that certain activities such as ballet, modeling, gymnastics, and wrestling often emphasize thinness, which puts your child more at risk for developing an eating disorder.
  - Encourage your child to find out which physical activities she enjoys, so she learns to exercise for enjoyment instead of to chase the perfect body.

- Promote a healthy lifestyle. Kids tend to pick up their parents' lifestyle habits, whether they are smoking, exercising, obsessing about dieting, or eating lots of sweets. Work toward moderation so they don't feel deprived, yet get the benefits of a well-rounded eating pattern.

Of course there are no guarantees, but these suggestions will help your daughter feel better about herself. Also keep in mind that many more boys and men are now falling prey to eating disorders.

By writing about the power mothers have on their daughters' self-esteem and body image issues, I hope women begin to understand the power of words to offer encouragement instead of despair. The seeds of negativity create weeds that lead to self-contempt.

But the seeds of encouragement offer joy as we learn to look at our bodies in terms of the amazing things they can do. Will you use your words to bless flowers of joy onto the next generation, or seeds of despair onto today's children and teens?

Yes, the wave of our cultural messages is beastly when it comes to body image. But there is always hope. We can, together, fight the Bandit and thrive. The messages may be Mama Mia sized, but we can turn the tide of change. We can fight the lies with the glory of truth. And this will create real and lasting change in the hearts of girls and women. We will not be swallowed by the power of the Body Image Bandit. God is on our side, and in the end the good always wins.

Chapter 12

Entering the Abyss of Eatingdisorderville

A university track star stood in the cafeteria line counting grains of rice to put on her plate. We have known for years that models and athletes – particularly gymnasts – often struggle with eating disorders. But the statistics for the American population as a whole are mind-boggling. Nearly 10 million females and 1 million males in the U.S. battle eating disorders such as anorexia and bulimia. Millions more suffer from binge eating disorder.

Puberty and late teen/early adult years are the most common stages of life to begin struggling with an eating disorder, but symptoms occur as young as kindergarten. Sometimes even earlier. This is partially the fallout of our poisonous culture which floods us with pictures of models of people who are airbrushed, photo shopped, and who probably do not menstruate due to a low body fat percentage.

Years ago when I swam several times a week, I remember a woman in her seventies who swam an hour and a half a day, seven days a week. I marveled at her dedication. But as I look back, I realize she was obsessed with her appearance and addicted to exercise. She obviously spent a great deal of time working on her makeup and hair before jumping into the pool. Every hair was in place and her eyes and lips outlined perfectly, as though she was attending a formal dinner instead of swimming. Most likely, she had bulimia. Not in the sense that she purged her food, but in the sense she could not live with herself if she did not religiously burn up a certain number of calories every day. People think of bulimia as purging, but a common aspect of bulimia is over exercising in an attempt to burn up calories from bingeing.

More than one in three dieters progresses to pathological dieting. What does this mean? They become so consumed with dieting that it develops into a cycle similar to the cycle of addiction. Saturating themselves with magazines and books about how to lose weight, they mirror the same habits as other addicts. Thoughts and images of losing weight dominate their thoughts as they pour over calorie, carbohydrate, and/or fat gram counters, envisioning how they will look with their new perfect bodies. But like any other relapse, they tend to gain more weight after each diet. They lose weight while dieting, but the ping pong dieting and then bingeing causes them to gain more after going off each diet.

One in four pre-adolescent cases of anorexia occurs in boys. Boys and men are starting to catch up with girls and women in regards to their obsessions with their bodies.

By now you probably understand more than ever how body image, weight, and food issues are more about our hearts and our stories than food, fat grams, and exercise. In other words, until we unveil the underlying issues that pull us into unhealthy relationships with food and body image, we won't win the war against the Body Image Bandit. Pain in our stories caused by life events such as break-ups and unhealthy relationships cause us to develop unhealthy relationships with food and our bodies.

Self-medicating with food is common, as we have discussed throughout our voyage. Unfortunately, so is comparing our bodies to airbrushed, photo-shopped images of concentration camp thin women. We have been brainwashed by many media sources into believing flawless is beautiful and achievable.

Bulimia often roars its head when a person experiences rejection. Because of our poisonous culture which worships thinness, the brainwashing of the ads and images kick into high gear and tell them, "If you were thinner, he wouldn't have left you." And so many girls and women plummet into the mucky mire by starving themselves, making a knee-jerk reaction of trying to lose weight.

As we discussed before, "Sticks and stones will break my bones but words will never hurt me," is one of the biggest lies on the planet. Words have the power to shoot bullets into our hearts and devour our self-worth. When faced with a rude comment about their bodies, many girls throw themselves into dieting, excessive exercising, and/or begin the cycle of purging when they get rejected.

When my friend Candy and I went on a hike, she told me of her struggle with bulimia from her late teens until her early thirties. Now in her early fifties, I invited her to share her story. She graciously explained she would be honored if it would help other people. Knowing many readers have been enticed by the beast of bulimia, I assured Candy others would gain courage and strength from her journey. They would understand that when darkness and despair envelop them, hope still prevails.

As we walked down the path through the evergreen woods, Candy told me about her background. "My parents argued a lot. They had a lot of fights – not physically, but my brother and I huddled together when they yelled." I was not surprised to hear this because bulimia is strongly related to control. When Candy's life felt out of control due to the yelling, she felt powerless.

People often deny their powerlessness because other people have it much worse. While that can be true, it is minimizing the problem and helps to deny the gravity of a situation. Living in a toxic environment is much more harmful than most people realize. It changes brain chemistry and causes damage to our immune systems. And just as weighty is the fact that it teaches us that yelling and screaming is normal and that is what relationships are like.

Then Candy explained her first romantic relationship. "It was never a good relationship," she continued. "I didn't have any good role models for relationships." Due to the rockiness of her parents' relationship, her own dating relationships were rocky. That is what she knew. Candy started dating Brad in her later high school years, and eventually they married and moved to Germany because he was in the Air Force. They were stationed in a remote village, so Candy felt isolated. She and Brad drank a lot each evening.

He picked on her and called her 'fat' although she wore a size 6. He was controlling and told her not to laugh or behave in certain ways. All this negativity squelched her and she withdrew inside herself.

Candy gained some weight because she was bored, depressed and isolated. She cried herself to sleep most nights. Brad said, "I will not tolerate an obese woman." He also often said, "You eat a lot." Eventually she began purging. She had a history of self-harm, and she viewed her bulimia as an extension of self-harm.

"All I could think about sometimes was throwing up, and threw up three to four times per day." The bulimia took over her thinking, and she was caught in a vortex of shame from bingeing and purging.

Eventually Candy gave birth, and while she nursed little Connie, Brad attempted to turn the mattress over on her. Another time he said something about going to get a gun, and so she left. That was the end of the abusive relationship.

She learned about abuse and bulimia and learned how to deal with the feelings which resulted in purging. Bulimia, in many ways, is really about purging feelings just as much as food. Often people grow up in homes where they are told things like, "Don't let ____ bother you. Just let it go." But as humans, we want to be validated and told, "I can understand why you feel like that." Feelings have to be released in healthy ways. If not, they stay inside us and lead to self-medication.

Candy eventually crawled out of the black hole of bulimia. She wishes she had received professional help back then, and she would advise anyone who struggles with bulimia to seek professional help. In those days help for eating disorders wasn't readily available. Candy expressed deep gratitude that God helped her out of Bulimiaville. Every once in a while she still feels an urge to purge, but she doesn't follow through with it because she figures out what is really eating at her.

Decades later, Candy is happily married to a kind, sweet man. Her three kids are doing well. One will graduate from college this year. Tears welled up in her eyes as she remembered the contrast of her old life and her new life. Several years ago, she asked Jesus to take control of her life and to forgive her of her sins. She told some people about her secret life of struggling with bulimia, and over time she was healed.

I don't want to over-simplify eating disorders, however. They are complex and eating disorder specialists offer many great approaches and techniques to treat such disorders. Please see the resources offered at the end of this chapter and pursue professional help if you're struggling with an eating disorder.

I asked Candy if she wanted to add anything else. She said, "Yes. There is help! Get professional help. You don't have to be this way forever."

Note: If you are in an abusive relationship, please get professional help. Do not use your own phone or electronic device because your partner could access your phone/internet history. Go to a library or use a different phone or computer than your own to access the National Domestic Violence Hotline at www.thehotline.org for help with domestic violence. 800-799-7233 or TTY 800-787-3224 are the National Domestic Violence Hotline numbers.

If you struggle with an eating disorder, please go to:

www.nationaleatingdisorders.org
www.aplaceofhope.com

Chapter 13

Beware of Drunk Monkeys

Guarding Your Heart

I once had a professor who said, "Trying to control your mind is like trying to control a room full of drunk monkeys." Although that isn't entirely true, we all have times when our thoughts grow unmanageable– somewhat like drunk monkeys.

Understanding Our Enemy

You know you've been bit by that pesky Body Image Bandit too many times to count. But just who is he? Let's unmask the Body Image Bandit so we can understand his tactics and can defend ourselves from him. His mission is to kill, steal, and destroy. Yet thankfully, God provides ways we can protect ourselves.

John 8:44 says, "He was a murderer from the

beginning, not holding to the truth, for there is no truth in him. When he lies, he speaks his native language, for he is a liar and the father of lies." That evil thief, the Body Image Bandit, wants to gobble you up for dinner with lies. Then he can discourage you so you will be distracted from God's true calling for your life. If you're busy worrying about your jean size, you'll never tap into your real mission in life.

Amazing. No wonder we drop into despair if we listen to his voice. The Bandit disguises himself as an angel of light, as 2 Corinthians 11:14 states: "And no wonder, for Satan himself masquerades as an angel of light." An example is when adolescents put a finger down their throats to make themselves throw up. Yet they pay a costly price as the lie entices them into a false sense of belief that purging is a gift.

If you suffer from bulimia, don't let the father of lies convince you that you'll never improve. That's another lie from the liar of liars! The enemy uses that lie to seal the gigantic envelope full of untruths he's fed you all these years.

How do we combat the lies? We fight the lies with – drumroll, please: Truth. Satan's weapon of choice is lies. So we fight his lies with the truth of God's Word. I'll say more about that in the next chapter, but before we get there, we need to learn to protect our minds from the monster – the Body Image Bandit.

Any time we find ourselves thinking these lies, we're being fed by lies from the pesky beast:

1. My worth is based on my appearance.

2. I'm not _____ enough. (Fill the blank with any of the following words, or other words that resonate: pretty, skinny, tall, etc.)

You're Being Brainwashed! Guard Your Heart above All Else

At the dawn of the computer era, computer programmers used to say, "Garbage in, garbage out." This meant if a computer received incorrect information, it produced errors. The same principle applies to our brains. If our minds take in trash, we think junky thoughts.

Is it any wonder we suffer from body image struggles? One reason is we don't protect our hearts well. The Bible commands us to shield our hearts in Proverbs 4:23. "Above all else, guard your heart, for it is the wellspring of life." Notice it says, "Above all else." What a powerful phrase. In other words, if we don't guard our hearts, we suffer weighty consequences. Engrave this verse on your heart!

This means we constantly guard against all images and ideas that derail us into despair. It's an epic task because we are bombarded with pictures and ideas from the media, including the Internet, television, movies, radio, phone and other devices. Add to that our conversations - including real, text and social media conversations. All together, we hear messages from hundreds of sources. We're drowning in a sea of lies, but we can learn to navigate the ocean with wisdom. Then we can rest peacefully in the Harbor of Hope.

If we let our guard down, the Body Image Bandit will sneak those poisonous lies into our heads. Protect your mind from the attacks of the Body Image Bandit! This involves shielding yourself from everything that causes you to compare your body, face, or other body parts with those of other people.

When asked on Facebook, "When are you most unhappy with your face, body, etc.?" women, men, and teens responded with the following struggles. I added "triggers" I've heard from clients and those I've experienced:

- **Mirrors**: This category includes all reflective services such as store windows.

- **Magazines:** Fashion, beauty, celebrity, women's, teen, fitness, and men's magazines.
- **Pictures (photographs or video footage) on any media such as pictures, movies, television shows, and advertisements.**

  -of *yourself*

  -of *models* (airbrushed and photo shopped)

-of *others* you consider more attractive.

- **Scales:** It's easy to get obsessed with scales so the number influences whether or not you have a good day.
- **Size tags:** These can cause stress if you listen to the lie of the Body Image Bandit that your value is based on a particular size.
- **Conversations:** Sometimes people feel sad or dejected due to "fat talk." This category includes any conversation centered on body size, body parts, ("My butt looks fat in these jeans," for example), weight, fat, diets, clothing sizes.

- **Others:** You may have other triggers.

We encounter triggers almost everywhere we go, so guarding our hearts is extremely difficult. Some triggers are easier to protect ourselves from than others. I'll teach you some techniques to shield your heart from the lies in a few minutes. But first you will need to identify your triggers.

> Try this: Make a list of your body image triggers over a 24-hour period. Then place an A beside those you think you can *realistically* avoid. Place a V by those you will "turn the volume down" on.

Although you probably know some of your triggers, writing them down will help you identify them. "Then you will know the truth, and the truth will set you free," Jesus said in John 8:32. The more we learn about the times, places, and things that drive our minds down Stinking Thinking Lane, the better we can protect ourselves from the lies of the Body Image Bandit.

The "Game" of Body Shame:

This game looks similar to the game of Monopoly, except on a much smaller scale. All players start on the square of shame. Your game piece is shaped like a pair of jeans.

Square 1. Shame:

You feel discouraged because you don't meet the photo-shopped, false concept of beauty promoted in our culture. You've experienced literally hundreds of thousands of pictures, film, and dialogues that programed your soul into believing you're not good enough. The barrage of messages flood your brain and heart into despair. Roll the dice and move to the next square.

Square 2: Diet

If you've landed on this square, it's probably Monday. ;) Roll the dice and wait your turn this round because you stepped on the scale and learned you gained three pounds over the weekend. Suck in your stomach because you're trying to pour yourself into the size of jeans you've always dreamed of wearing. Roll the dice. Move to the next step.

Square 3: Fail

You go off your diet. Of course you did, because you set yourself up for failure by going "on" a diet. Although he wasn't referring to dieting, Paul described his struggle of doing what he despised in Romans 7:15–16: "My own behavior baffles me. For I find myself doing what I really hate, and not doing what I really want to do," (Living Bible). Roll the dice and go to the mall. Oops, it finally happened – you busted the rear-end seam of your "magic size" jeans. Roll the dice and open your bottom drawer to pull out your old jeans.

Square 4: Binge

You eat everything except the TV - although you wonder if it would taste ok with chocolate sauce on top! Look at fashion or celebrity magazines while you wait in the dentist's waiting area. Roll the dice, and if they add up to an even number, you fall into a trap called bulimia.

Square 5: Promise

You've landed on a square that says, "Pick a card from the blue stack." The blue cards are shaped like jeans. The card you choose says, "You've gained 4 pounds and you feel desperate. So you promise yourself to go on yet another diet … on Monday. You spend ¼ of your last paycheck on a ride called the Diet Roller Coaster. You often feel hopeful on the ride. But like a disappointed child, the ride ends sooner than expected. You feel discouraged and irritated the weight you lost on your diet ended within six weeks.

Square 6: Repeat these steps until you're more done than a burnt roast!

Sally, a twenty-something woman in college, attends a party where she meets a guy named Bill. She's always wanted to talk to him but never had the opportunity. The conversation flows and Sally can tell Bill is interested in her.

Then Cari joins the conversation. She is beautiful, and soon Sally feels the conversation is primarily between Cari and Bill. She decides to leave the conversation. Her heart aches to be beautiful like Cari. Sally asks herself, *How can I measure up?*

While driving home, her mind slides into the gutter of self-contempt. She makes a vow to go on a diet ... on Monday.

Since she's planning to diet, Sally gives herself permission to binge until the magic day of Monday.

She binges the rest of the weekend, gorging herself on burgers, fries, milkshakes, candy, and pasta. This leads to more sadness and shame. As you can see, when Sally jumped on the bandwagon of all-or-nothing thinking, she began her descent into discouragement.

I love this verse and try to repeat it to myself when I first feel discouraged: "Have I not commanded you? Be strong and courageous. Do not be afraid; do not be discouraged, for the LORD your God will be with you wherever you go," (Joshua 1:9). Write it down and put it in your kitchen window sill, or on your mirror.

Cycle:

1. Comparing

2. Shame

3. All-or-Nothing Thinking

4. Dieting, Purging, Over-Exercising, and/or Purchasing Radical products/services

5. Shame due to eating "bad" foods or failure to lose weight, etc.

6. Using props (scale, clothing tag sizes, mirrors,

"fat talk" conversations) to judge if you look better or worse.

7. Repeat.

Now that you know your triggers, you're ready to learn how to use the "Avoid" or "Volume" techniques to kick those lies of the Body Image Bandit to the curb!

Let me explain how you can practice the avoidance or volume techniques in your day-to-day living. You may be able to avoid magazines that display photos of women who appear flawless, to a certain extent. I choose not to purchase such magazines. I rarely open them. One way to do this is learning to bounce your eyes. This means you immediately look at something else. Let's say you're in the mall and you walk by a display window. You begin to feel discouraged because the mannequins are thin. You can choose to bounce your eyes away and look at the floor or a shoe display in another window. (Ahhhh... the power of shoes!)

Guarding Your Heart from the Body Image Bandit

The most effective strategies for guarding your

heart are:

> **1. Total Avoidance:** This means you avoid the triggers as much as possible. But many times you can't avoid them altogether. In this case, you:
>
> **2. Turn down the "volume":** This means you limit your exposure.

Which triggers will you be able to avoid? Which will you need to turn the volume down on? Let's take your scale, for example. Is your scale a friend, a nag, or an enemy? How many times have you stepped on it the past week? If you feel as though your scale owns you, then you're obsessing about your weight and it probably makes things worse.

Now let's ask some questions about mirrors. This is a tough category for me. Sometimes I check the mirror many times throughout the day. The thing is – I probably don't look much different than the last time I checked myself. So I'm going to challenge myself to "turn down the volume" on how much I look at myself.

The next category is pictures. When you see your pictures, do you tend to compare yourself to friends and other people?

Now you know the subtle ways those drunk monkeys try to control your thinking. You're onto them – and on your way to a more joyful life, free of stinking thinking! With God's help, you can learn to guard your heart by keeping those drunk monkeys at bay. You will experience new freedom as you spend your time leaning into your true calling instead of battling drunk monkeys.

Chapter 14

Recognize, Reject, and Replace the Lies of the Body Image Bandit

As I mentioned in the previous chapter, the first step of defeating the Body Image Bandit is to guard our hearts. The next steps are to recognize, reject, and replace the lies of that rascal Bandit. We'll examine each of these separately.

Step 1: Guard Your Heart

(Read the previous chapter if you haven't already.)

Step 2: Recognize the Lies

If you're plummeting into despair about your body, chances are you've bitten into a tall tale of the Body Image Bandit. The lies of the enemy can be hard to separate from truth because they become normal – a part of our thoughts. They tangle within the truths like a weed tangles around a flower.

For example, remember the scene I described earlier where I sat in a circle with other women? I'd noticed my thighs looked larger than the woman's seated next to me. What I didn't tell you is I was wearing size 8 jeans.

The Bandit convinced me my thighs were fat, which led to feelings of shame. But when I reflected on my thinking process, I realized my thoughts cascaded into a waterfall of negativity. And it all happened in less than a minute!

When I compare myself with other people (real or those on a computer screen or in magazines), I'm stepping into a lie from the Bandit.

Satan is slick. He deceives us by distorting and twisting truth. Satan is a thief. He steals our joy and derails our thoughts to discourage us. He ambushes us with lies so we wallow in self-pity. Then we can't move forward with the tasks God created us to do. Also, we will drop into the depths of despair. According to John 10:10, "The thief comes only to steal and kill and destroy; I came that they may have life, and have it abundantly."

Just as a waterfall flows downward into a pool or another water source, your thought processes plunge if you permit a lie to rent space in your head.

Here are some common lies of the Body Image Bandit:

- I am ugly.

- My _____ is/are ugly.

(face, eyes, waist, thighs, etc.)

- I am unworthy/worthless.

- I am not good enough. (Body parts too small, large, skin is too light, dark, etc.)

- I am too _____

(Tall, short, fat, etc.).

- I am unlovable.

- I am shameful (bad).

Any thoughts of your value coming from your appearance are lies! The trickster, the Body Image Bandit, is filling your head with despair.

Learn to recognize the Bandit's lies. Keep in mind they are often subtle and hard to identify. Always remember, as we already discussed, that

Satan disguises himself as an angel of light. Think of it as though you are a guard, and your job is to tackle each lie the second it enters your mind.

For example, in line at the movies, you notice the woman in front of you. You catch yourself wondering what size she wears, or you think she is thinner or prettier than you. Or your comparison results in a belief you are skinnier or prettier. Once again, you've fallen prey to the con artist Bandit.

Comparing is a form of coveting, which God warns against. In the Old Testament, God warned the people not to covet. Covet means to long for something belonging to someone else. Deuteronomy 5:21 says, "You shall not covet your neighbor's wife. You shall not set your desire on your neighbor's house or land, his male or female servant, his ox or donkey, or anything that belongs to your neighbor." God knew coveting would lead down Negative Lane, into a cesspool of thoughts to culminate in radical behavior such as greed and stealing.

The same warning applies to body image. If we covet someone else's body, we begin to take drastic measures in attempt to become prettier so we can fill the holes in our hearts.

The battle is spiritual. The Bandit will convince you that you are ugly, bad, fat, shameful, and worthless, that nobody would want you, and so on.

The trick is to catch the lie as soon as it enters your head! Here are some common examples:

- You're at a party and feel discouraged because another girl or guy is thinner.
- A person of the opposite sex is talking to someone you've always wanted to hang out with. You feel less attractive than her.
- You run into friends at the mall, and they introduce you to someone. You feel threatened because their complexion appears flawless and your skin is breaking out.
- A new person joins your class, and he or she looks like a model. You're deeply jealous.
- Another person comments on how beautiful your sister or friend or Mom or cousin is.

Try this: Keep a log of the lies you believe for a day. Record the lie, and what you were doing when you first noticed it. Remember, lies are often tough to identify, so you may need a trusted friend or therapist to help you. This will help you determine when your thinking derails.

Prayer: Jesus, please give me wisdom to know exactly when a lie enters my head, and what the lie is, and help me to replace all lies with your truth. In Jesus' name, Amen.

Step 3: Reject the Lies

The *second* you catch a lie from the Body Image Bandit, picture a sign that says, "No parking any time."

```
┌─────────────────────────┐
│                         │
│      NO PARKING         │
│                         │
│      ANY TIME           │
│                         │
└─────────────────────────┘
```

Practice, practice, practice!

Due to the amount of media we're exposed to, lies pour into our heads at a much greater pace than they did years ago.

We need to constantly filter our minds. If we see and listen to texts, movies, shows, radio, friends on social media sites that send our minds down Negative Lane, of course we will feel discouraged, unworthy, and shameful.

> "We demolish arguments and every pretension which sets
> itself up against the knowledge of God, and we take
> captive every thought to make it obedient to Christ."
> 2 Corinthians 10:5

Shame gives birth to radical all-or-nothing thinking. In other words, dieting which leads to bingeing, which leads to shame, which leads back to the cycle again. So in order to break the cycle, we need to reject the lies. Don't forget the "No Parking Any Time" sign, and this life-changing verse:

Copy this verse and place it on your bathroom mirror or another strategic place to remind yourself to take each thought captive. Notice the verse says to demolish. "We *demolish* arguments and every pretension that sets itself up against the knowledge of God, and we take captive every thought to make it obedient to Christ" (Note: Italics and bold are my own). The word "demolish," is monumental. We must rid ourselves of all lies completely. When we annihilate the arguments and pretensions, we cut the lies off at their source. Period.

Why does the Bible tell us to take our thoughts captive? Because once a lie sneaks in, it can gobble up your healthy thinking until your brain is a big pile of untruths. You'll be drowning in a lake of shame so deep you can't step forward to follow God's calling on your life. Besides that, you'll be paralyzed with shoots of despair firing darts into your heart.

Step 4: Replace the Lies

Imagine you click on your TV remote. You channel surf until you find a show. But a few minutes later, you realize you don't like it. So you change the channel.

Think about your thought process the same way. When you notice your thought patterns behaving like drunk monkeys, choose to change them. Remember the phrase, "Change channels."

Romans 12:2 says, "Do not conform any longer to the pattern of this world, but be transformed by the renewing of your mind. Then you will be able to test and approve what God's will is – his good, pleasing and perfect will."

What transforms our thoughts? Studying the Bible, memorizing specific verses relating to our struggles, and pulling them out of our hearts when needed. In other words, we change the channel from the Lie channel to the Truth channel. But in order to do this, we must become aware of our thoughts at all times. A phrase to ask ourselves is, *"What channel are my thoughts on?"*

"I praise you because I am fearfully and

wonderfully made; your works are wonderful, I know that full well." Psalm 139:14 reminds me I'm created in God's image and I'm a masterpiece.

Another verse that helps to focus my heart on what's truly important is this: "The Lord does not look at the things people look at. People look at the outward appearance, but the Lord looks at the heart." 1Samuel 16:7b steers my mind on course when it behaves like a room full of drunk monkeys.

Just as your TV offers different shows, you have a few options about which "shows" to select on your channels:

Let's look at some specific verses for dealing with lies that trick our minds into believing we're not good enough. Decide which ones you struggle with, and copy them onto paper. Then you can place them in strategic locations to quickly reframe your thinking. The faster you identify the "stinking thinking" channels and switch to positive channels, the better you will feel. You'll spend less time obsessing about your appearance, which will allow you more time to be the salt and light in this shadowy world. We'll call this channel the Truth Channel.

Verses for specific lies:

LIE: Beauty is extremely important.

TRUTH: What matters most is not your outer appearance – the styling of your hair, the jewelry you wear, the cut of your clothes – but your inner disposition. (1 Peter 3:3, MSG)

LIE: Appearance is almost everything.

TRUTH: "But the fruit of the spirit is love, joy, peace, patience, kindness, goodness, faithfulness, and self-control." (Galatians 5:22)

LIE: The thinner, the better.

TRUTH: Proverbs 31, the classic passage on womanhood, says, "Her arms are strong for her tasks." This implies she isn't ultra-thin.

LIE: Food is the enemy, as it creates fat.

TRUTH: God created a variety of foods to enjoy in moderation to nourish our bodies. "For everything God created is good, and nothing is to be rejected it if is received with thanksgiving." (1 Timothy 4:4)

LIE: Our culture tells us we can do whatever we want to our bodies.

TRUTH: God creates masterpieces using new canvasses each time. "Offer your bodies as living sacrifices, holy and pleasing to God – this is your spiritual act of worship." (Romans 12:1).

LIE: Youth is beautiful, old age is ugly. (Although, thankfully, many cultures value the elderly much greater than most westernized cultures.)

TRUTH: But the Bible tells us older people are wiser and have more life experience. "Gray hair is a crown of splendor; it is attained by a righteous life." (Proverbs 16:31).

I've outlined the edges of my bathroom mirror with Bible verses. Those verses keep me grounded in remembering who I really am, and what I'm really about. In other words, I am a masterpiece, designed with a body, face, personality and story. I can use my gifts, talents, and appearance to make the world a better place, or I can entangle myself in the web created by a culture saturated with images and negative messages about how I "should" look. If I stumble on lies from the Bandit, I'll feel discouraged. But if I choose to identify the lies and replace them with scripture, I can live out God's true calling on my life. After all, I wasn't created to obsess about my appearance. I was designed by a loving God who is creating a glorious quilt for my life.

Some days are harder than others, as far as identifying and replacing lies are concerned. I'm still working on this process of catching my thoughts as soon as I detect them. I would be lying if I pretended never struggle. Yet I rejoice because I'm much better at it than I used to be. I can choose to turn my thoughts upward in a spirit of gratitude and thankfulness, or inward into self-pity.

The Power Tool of Praise

Thankfully, we have a power tool that is always available to us! We can praise God even when we are in a downward spiral.

Remember the No Parking Any Time sign, and turn your attention on thanking Jesus for everything you are thankful for (unrelated to body image). What are you thankful for? I know you may want to skip this and continue reading, but I encourage you to write a gratitude list. This will help you remember to "change channels" to the positive when you are feeling discouraged about your body or your life.

Sometimes I forget to do this, but it works! Like many activities, we improve with practice. ·

Please copy the verses that address the body image issues you struggle with. Then memorize them. Don't gloss over this part. There is no substitute for this! Hebrews 4:12 says, "For the word of God is alive and active. Sharper than any double-edged sword, it penetrates even to dividing soul and spirit, joints and marrow; it judges the thoughts and attitudes of the heart."

Sometimes we forget or feel too busy to memorize verses. Or believe it's something little kids do in Sunday school. We suffer with Satan's continual infliction of flooding our minds with shame due to body image issues; yet we forget we have the power of God at our fingertips! "I have hidden your word in my heart that I might not sin against you," says Psalm 119:11. Do you see how powerful this verse is?

You are an amazing treasure, and when you hop on the shame train, thinking, "Oh, if only I was a size ___, then my life would be great!" Seriously? The problem with that statement is everywhere you go, there you are. All the struggles in your heart will still be there because your food and body image issues are about your life story – pain seeping inside your soul. If you treat only the symptom, the pain in your soul will pop up in other ways.

I know that just as the Lord provides physicians and naturopaths, he provides trained therapists. We are trained to see patterns, styles of relating and thinking that create chaos in our lives. You can't see the picture when you're in it. I used to believe we only needed the Bible to help us with our problems. I passionately study the Bible and try to read through it every year. And I am also grateful for the therapists

God has used to heal the pain in my own story. Since 400 styles of counseling now exist, finding the right fit can be challenging. That's why it's important to try a therapist five or six times before changing to another.

We live in a scarred world, so we must continue to guard our hearts and fight the lies of the Body Image Bandit. Otherwise our brains will fill up with garbage. Then we will plummet into despair and feel as though our heads are saturated with a sea of lies. Then – and only then – can we become the people we were created to be.

Chapter 15

Dance Your Life Song like a Diva

Some mornings I drag myself out of bed, wash my face in the bathroom sink, and think, *I look like a rat that's been drug out of a hole backwards.* My hair looks like it's glued to my head, and if I accidentally get a whiff of my armpits, whew! Those little innocent things could be used as weapons. (Thank you, hot flashes!) Dark half-moons adorn my eyes, with specks of eyeliner sitting on top of them like sprinkles on a cupcake. A crease line from my pillowcase leaves its imprint on my cheek. Those mornings, I don't feel I feel I have any calling except grabbing a cup of coffee and slapping some deodorant on my pits so I don't make anyone pass out.

At those times, I don't feel like a diva. But the truth is I am a masterpiece, and so are you! I remind myself who I am as a precious princess in God's sight when I reach that soggy undergrowth space inside my head. I tell myself I'm an original, made in God's image to do specific tasks he's created me for. How exciting is that?

What if you could embrace life as if you were a well-designed diva, a glorious piece of art, created to accomplish specific things? The Bible says that *is* what you are. Your life has purpose and meaning. There is much more to your timeline than asking if your jeans make you look fat! God didn't create you to spend day after day focusing on how to make your cheekbones appear higher, your eyes look bigger, or your waist look smaller. He has another vision for you, and he passionately invites you to climb on board.

Ephesians 2:10 says, "For we are God's handiwork, created in Christ Jesus to do good works, which God prepared in advance for us to do." Notice it does *not* say, "For we are God's workmanship, created in Christ Jesus to obsess about our tooshies, food, and how to get skinny." We were crafted for a much greater purpose. So hop off the scale, stop craning your neck to check out your tooshie, and get on with life! Only then can you discover and embrace your true calling – and dance your life song like a diva.

If you don't understand what your life song is, that's okay. If we back up to Ephesians 2:8–9, we learn we are saved by grace. "For it is by grace you have been saved, through faith—and this is not from yourselves, it is the gift of God- not by works, so that no one can boast."

This means we can't get to heaven by doing good things, which is the major difference between Christianity and other religions. In other words, we can't get to heaven by visiting sick people or baking cookies for the neighbors. We are saved simply by grace, through the blood of Jesus on the cross. Jesus died to pay the price of our sins because they separate us from God. He is holy – in other words set apart and absolutely perfect.

Yet we are all imperfect. All we have to do is ask him for forgiveness, and to take control of our lives. Once we do this, we are new creatures. Yet to learn and grow, we must study the Bible. If you're not familiar with it, get yourself one and begin by reading. Start in John. If you would rather read a free version, go to biblegateway.com and look at the NIV. Or if you have a smart phone, download the You Version app.

This doesn't mean our lives will be perfect, though. We live in a scuffed up, tainted world. Jesus promised in John 16:33, "I have told you these things so that in me you may have peace. In this world you will have trouble. But take heart! I have overcome the world."

Ephesians 2:10 gives me peace because I know I'm one-of-a-kind. God designed me with a unique story, personality, physical characteristics, and passions. Each chapter of my story happened for a reason, so I would be prepared for my calling. Even the darkest colors of my journey shaped my personality, forming a kaleidoscope of color and beauty. Many times I didn't understand the reasons for the pain. I do know, though, in the end all the highlights and lowlights will work together in the symphony of my life song.

Living on Maui as one of only a handful of white students in a public school provided me the opportunity to live as a minority. Growing up in several small towns in Washington State, I wouldn't have learned about the Hawaiian, Japanese, Chinese, Filipino, and Samoan cultures.

The prejudice I experienced as a sixth grader on Maui crescendoed into a despair so dark I had a plan to take my life. But now I understand the experience created a compost which formed a lovely, fruitful garden. As Romans 5:1–5 says, "Therefore, since we have been justified through faith, we have peace with God through our Lord Jesus Christ, through whom we have gained access by faith into this grace in which we now stand. And we boast in the hope of the glory of God. *Not only so, but we also glory in our sufferings, because we know that suffering produces perseverance; perseverance, character; and character, hope* (Italics mine). And hope does not put us to shame, because God's love has been poured out into our hearts through the Holy Spirit, who has been given to us." This scripture helps me understand everything happens for a reason, and even difficult experiences work to glorify God.

Don't you feel great peace to grasp the fact God created you as a special agent, to complete unique assignments while here on earth? And obsessing about "getting skinny" is not one of the assignments! Yes, you're an amazing work of art.

You aren't on the planet just to pass your days or fill your life with fun, fun, fun. Not that fun is a bad thing, because God invented fun. God holds the patent on fun. The Garden of Eden was certainly the most fun place on earth until the fruit incident in Genesis 3. Even though God created Eden, he didn't create us only to have fun. His purpose is grander than the Grand Canyon is deep and wide. He desires that each person come to know him in a real, life-changing way. And the exciting part is we each play roles in the phenomenal life movie.

God desires our hearts to radically transform due to a rich relationship with Jesus. This doesn't include room for obsessing about appearance. To care about our appearance is one thing, and to treat our bodies like they are temples of God is important. First Corinthians 6:19 says, "Do you not know that your body is a temple of the Holy Spirit, who is in you, whom you have received from God? You are not your own ..." But to fixate on appearance and spend inordinate amounts of time trying to look skinny or flawless is contrary to God's plan. We may celebrate our femininity and make the most out of our features. But if we go overboard and focus more on our appearance than what truly matters, we make beauty an idol.

First Timothy 4:8 says, "For physical training is of some value, but godliness has value for all things, holding promise for both the present life and the life to come." It took a while for that verse to sink under my skin, but now I try to live out the verse.

Since our bodies are temples of God, exercising provides ample benefits. Many studies have proven the value of exercise, and most Americans don't get enough exercise. So if you aren't exercising enough (or exercising at all), maybe a realistic goal is to work on finding exercise you enjoy so you can achieve a healthier lifestyle. If you don't enjoy it, chances are you won't be able to keep it up as a major life change. Keep looking until you discover something you like. If you try hard and still can't find anything, choose the one that gives you the least grief. Sometimes getting an exercise partner can make the task more pleasant and provide accountability as well.

So ... what *were* you created for? What is your life song? Maybe you have flitted about in life, not really understanding your purpose. Or maybe you have seen your value in terms of your outside appearance instead of the treasured, multi-faceted person God created you to be. Perhaps you feel lost and confused because you haven't discovered exactly what "good works" God created you to do. Sometimes I wish God would just email me or put a sticky note on my fridge to let me know exactly what to do! But that isn't how he works.

The beauty is God promises to give us wisdom if we ask him for it. James 1:5 says, "If any of you lacks wisdom, he should ask God, who gives generously to all without finding fault, and it will be given to him." That comforts me because all we need to do is ask! If you are confused or uncertain about your calling, ask

God to reveal it to you. Often we have more than one purpose and they may change at different times of our lives. I encourage you to take some time and pray diligently about your calling. Another idea is to go on a solitary retreat with your Bible and journal. Worship God, and pray diligently for him to reveal your life missions to you. Listen when people say you're good at something.

Remember though, your true calling will always line up with the Bible. If you believe something is your calling, and it's contrary to the Bible, it isn't your calling after all.

Often our mission statements – what we are called to do – center on the heart ache in our stories. Second Corinthians 1:3–4 says, "Praise be to the God and Father of our Lord Jesus Christ, the Father of compassion and the God of all comfort, who comforts us in all our troubles, so that we can comfort those in any trouble with the comfort we ourselves receive from God."

Tanya, a hairdresser who attends my church, is a fun, lovely woman. One day she felt God calling her to bake cupcakes for her neighbors. She didn't know them well, but wanted to bless them with her baking and invite them to see the movie, "Heaven is for Real." The family behind the true story will visit our church soon for an Eternity Conference, and she wanted to invite her neighbors to the event. People love Tanya's baking, so she realized she could use her talents to bless them. She provided movie tickets for the Heaven is for Real movie, as well as the book for each household along with the cupcakes.

One young man read the book in a day. He is looking forward to attending the conference at our church. Since Tanya delivered the packages, the neighbors visit and help each other more.

Shortly after delivering the cupcakes, she received $500.00 totally unexpected from a friend. This was a gift for referring him real estate clients over the years. "That was really a God thing," she said, as she explained how the money surprised her and covered the expenses for the neighborhood gifts.

Tanya demonstrates a beautiful example of how someone uses her gifts and talents to focus on what truly matters.

One of my best friends, Sherri, from Ohio, lived a party lifestyle in her teens. During her partying years, she had alias identities, used drugs and drank excessively. Eventually she moved in with her abusive boyfriend. One day Sherri decided she'd had enough. She left her abuser carefully so as to not leave a trail he could follow. This involved ditching her car so he wouldn't find her.

Sherri mailed a box of clothes to her grandmother's house in Washington state, and then hitch-hiked across the country to leave her abuser. (I'm definitely not recommending this strategy because of the danger, but this is part of her story.)

When she arrived in Washington, Sherri lived with relatives who facilitated a Bible study every week in their home. At first she hung out in her room during Bible study, avoiding the Jesus people. Eventually she gave up and began to build relationships with them, and ultimately invited Jesus to forgive her for her sins and take control of her life.

Sherri worked her way through nursing school. She worked in a hospital where she cared for babies born addicted to crack cocaine. Sherri later served on a mission trip on a ship, travelling to Africa to help perform surgeries.

Eventually she enrolled in Multnomah Seminary and earned a certificate in Bible. For many years she worked at a facility with teen girls addicted to drugs. She shared Christ with them as well as helped them on their journeys of recovery. The kids connected with her and greatly respected her honesty, her caring heart, and also - of all things - her ability to beat most of them at pool! She had become a pool expert while bar hopping in her earlier years. So God used Sherri's story to carve out her mission in life – at least one of the missions God specially designed her for. She understood the girls' hearts and stories, cared for and respected each of them.

God clearly said he created us as individual masterpieces in his sight for specific jobs. How cool is that?! (Ephesians 2:10) While we flit about devoting excessive time and energy to appearance, we focus on the fluff and not the substance.

I invite you to dance to your life song like a diva. Begin the new journey of discovering your life song, which is your true calling. Think, pray, and write about your natural talents, and your story. God designed you not to obsess, but to bless others with the music. So get rid of your scale, step away from the mirror and dance your life song like a diva.